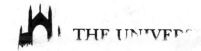

DEATH LITURGY AND RITUAL VOLUME I

At the beginning of the twenty-first century, the Christian Church continues to minister to the dying and the bereaved. However, it does so in a rapidly changing world. The traditional understandings of death and life after death are challenged by the disciplines of medicine, the law, philosophy, psychology and anthropology.

This two-volume study of Christian funerary theology and practice presents an invaluable account of funeral rites and the central issues involved for compilers and users. The author writes from direct experience of conducting funerals and of drafting liturgical resources for others.

In Volume I, Dr Sheppy argues that the Church ought to construct its theological agenda in dialogue with other fields of study. He argues for a Christian statement about death that finds its basis in the Paschal Mystery, since human death must be explained by reference to Jesus' death, descent to the dead, and resurrection. Using the three phases of van Gennep's theory of rites of passage, the author shows how the Easter triduum may be seen as normative for Christian liturgies of death.

Volume II reviews a wide range of current Christian funeral rites and examines how they reflect both the Church's concern for the death and resurrection of Christ and the contemporary secular demand for funerals which celebrate the life of the deceased.

PAUL SHEPPY is a Baptist minister in pastoral charge of a congregation in Reading, England. From 1987 to 2002 he was a member of the Joint Liturgical Group of Great Britain, serving as its Secretary from 1994. During the latter period, he was a member of the English Language Liturgical Consultation. He has been a member of the Churches' Funerals Group since 1997 and continues to serve as a Trustee of the Joint Liturgical Group.

LITURGY, WORSHIP AND SOCIETY

This new series comes at a time of great change in liturgy and much debate concerning traditional and new forms of worship, the suitability and use of places of worship, and wider issues concerning the interaction of liturgy, worship and contemporary society. Offering a thorough grounding in the historical and theological foundations of liturgy, books in the series explore and challenge many key issues of worship and liturgical theology which are currently in hot debate – issues set to make a significant impact on the place of the church in contemporary society. Presenting an ecumenical range of books, comparing and contrasting liturgical practices and concerns within various traditions and faiths, this series will appeal to those in university and theological colleges; adult education colleges; those on other ministry or lay ministry training courses; and practitioners and those involved in worship in churches across a broad ecumenical range.

Forthcoming titles in the series include

Inculturation of Christian Worship
Exploring the Eucharist
Phillip Tovey

West Syrian Liturgical Theology
Baby Varghese

Rituals and Theologies of Christian Baptism
Beyond the Jordan
Bryan D. Spinks

Daily Liturgical Prayer
Origins and Theory
Gregory W. Woolfenden

Death Liturgy and Ritual
Volume I

A Pastoral and Liturgical Theology

PAUL P.J. SHEPPY

ASHGATE

Published by
Ashgate Publishing Limited
Gower House
Croft Road
Aldershot
Hants GU11 3HR
England

Ashgate Publishing Company
Suite 420
101 Cherry Street
Burlington, VT 05401-4405
USA

Ashgate website: http://www.ashgate.com

British Library Cataloguing in Publication Data
Sheppy, Paul
    Death liturgy and ritual
    Vol. I: A pastoral and liturgical theology. – (Liturgy, worship and society)
    1.Death – Religious aspects – Christianity 2.Liturgics
    3.Funeral rites and ceremonies
    I.Title
    265.8'5

Library of Congress Cataloging-in-Publication Data
Sheppy, Paul P.J.
    Death liturgy and ritual / Paul P.J. Sheppy.
        p. cm. – (Liturgy, worship and society series)
    Includes bibliographical references and index.
    Contents: v. I. A pastoral and liturgical theology.
    ISBN 0-7546-0579-5 (alk. paper) – ISBN 0-7546-0580-9 (pbk. : alk. paper)
        1. Funeral service. 2. Death–Religious aspects–Christianity. I. Title. II. Series.

BV199.F8S53 2003
265'.85–dc21

2003052240

ISBN 0 7546 0579 5 (Hbk)
ISBN 0 7546 0580 9 (Pbk)

Printed and bound in Great Britain by MPG Books Ltd, Bodmin, Cornwall

To my wife and our daughter and son
and to the memory of my parents I dedicate this volume.

To Sue, Claire and Justin

To Philip and Odette

Contents

Acknowledgements

Books do not just happen. This book certainly has not. Many people have combined to help me in writing it; among them have been funeral directors and officiants, liturgists, the dying and the bereaved. There have been the congregations of which I have been privileged to be part and the communities in which I have lived. Simply to tell someone that you are interested in death produces some sort of interest – even if only a confirmation of your oddity!

To some friends, however, a special word of thanks should be spoken. The members of the Department of Theology and Religious Studies at the University of Leeds nurtured me in my doctoral research; to Al McFadyen and Philip Mellor I owe an enormous debt. Colleagues in Societas Liturgica have offered me opportunities to present papers to liturgical scholars for comment and correction; to Donald Gray, Robert Gribben and Richard Rutherford, I offer particular thanks. The Churches' Group on Funerals at Cemeteries and Crematoria has provided me with knowledgeable and encouraging friends who have urged me on when otherwise I might have faltered; Peter Jupp, John Lampard and Geoffrey Rowell have inspired with their own tireless studies as well as their kindly words.

To Sarah Lloyd, the series editor, and the team at Ashgate I owe the debt of time – I have delayed for too long and yet still have asked for more. They have been generosity itself. Betty Brown read the complete text before I sent it to the publishers. She saved me from more errors than I imagined possible, and I can only apologise to her that there was so much for her to do.

Beyond these, additional words must be said. To those closest to me – my wife and our daughter and son, who have put up with death and funerals, waking and sleeping – what can I say? "Sorry," seems far too little.

CHAPTER 1

Introduction to Volume I

The contemporary milieu and a personal reflection on methodology

At the beginning of the twenty-first century funeral rites in much of the Western world face a crisis. This crisis springs from a variety of factors: the changing nature of belief about death and what (if anything) lies beyond; the change in many places from burial to cremation as the predominant means of disposal; the loss of communal customs and practices in the massive shift to urbanization; and the experience (particularly in Britain) of the twenty-minute "funeral slot" in which the ritual agenda is expected to be completed.[1] These constraints are increasingly assumed and those officiating at funerals have to manage the ritual event in circumstances unimaginable to those of previous generations.

Christian liturgists, who inherit traditions shaped by the theologies and social customs of nearly two thousand years, have a number of choices as they attempt to respond to this emerging situation.

A conservative approach would be to change nothing – apart, perhaps, from some modernisation of the language. On such a view, the unchanging truth of Christian faith stands secure in the midst of the maelstrom. In all the uncertainty, the liturgy points safely and unswervingly where it has always pointed.

> Change and decay in all around I see,
> O Thou, who changest not, abide with me.[2]

At the other end of the scale we might find an approach to death that abandons traditional Christian theology. Those adopting such a line might argue that Christian theology was predominantly shaped in a pre-modern world. Where it failed to accept the challenges of modernity, it came to be perceived as increasingly irrelevant – even untrue. *A fortiori*, a similar (but greater) fate awaits any theology that fails to embrace the post modernist analysis.

It may not surprise the reader to discover that having drawn these two boundaries I want to argue a case somewhere in the middle. In the course of this book I shall try to

---

[1] Mary Douglas. 1996. *Natural Symbols: explorations in cosmology* (London: Routledge, 2nd edition) argues that the pejorative use of ritual to mean "empty ritual", or a series of actions undertaken by one who lacks commitment to any underlying meaning, prejudices discussion and disables effective debate with those from other disciplines in the social sciences. "Ritual" in what follows (unless otherwise specifically qualified) will adopt the definition offered by Douglas: "action and beliefs in the symbolic order without reference to the commitment or non-commitment of the actors" (1996: 2).

[2] Perhaps it is not entirely coincidental that in England, when hymns are sung at funerals, this continues to be a strong favourite. The popularity of *Abide with me* remains because it is well known as a result of its use at the FA Cup Final. However, it is noticeable that this is less the case than it was even twenty years ago. Fewer people sing the hymn on that occasion, and it frequently fights a losing battle with the chants and team songs of the rival groups of supporters.

respond to contemporary understandings of the world, since I share the view that theology has to engage with the same world that we all inhabit and experience. At the same time, I shall not assume that the insights of other disciplines leave no room for theological reflection and critique. As a Christian minister committed to theological and liturgical engagement, I regard the story of Jesus as central (though not exclusive) in God self-disclosure; and as a Christian believer and worshipper, I make best sense of the world through the Christian story of faith. This is not an understanding shared by the majority of people today – nor has it ever been. Yet, in the words of Martin Luther's great affirmation, "Here I stand, I can do no other".

From earliest times human beings have marked death by solemn observance in funeral rites. Our contemporary dilemma is that the religious associations with death are less commonly adhered to in the West than they have been in the past. Most mourners attending a funeral will expect the service to provide a summary of the deceased's life; the Christian officiant, invited to take the funeral, will have an additional – even different – agenda. For the Christian death is not simply a closure, it is a gateway to something new. The Christian does not simply look back; death provides an opportunity for hope. It is a call not simply to review what has happened, it is a call also to anticipate the resurrection.

This book will address death from theological and liturgical perspectives, but will do so on the understanding that theology and liturgy are never isolated activities. Theology is inevitably an exercise within or over against tradition; as such it is an engagement with others as well as with God. Liturgy is equally a communal experience; beyond the texts lies the worship of the Christian community.[3] Even the hermit prays in community, for prayer is made in company with the saints of every time and place. Nonetheless, this book is a confessional pilgrimage. I cannot travel alone and yet no one else can make my journey for me – even though they make it with me. I travel to death, and I shall die my death.[4]

This bipolarity between the communitarian nature of academic debate and personal nature of one's mortality will be expressed by the device of engaging with the work of colleagues in a variety of disciplines while writing in the first person. We shall need to understand the insights of those who examine death from within the life and social sciences. In hearing what they say, we shall need to ask how their questions and conclusions impinge on the concerns of theology and liturgy. From such discourse, I hope to suggest both a theoretical framework and some practical applications for the funeral liturgist. These proposals will not be in the nature of final conclusions, but will carry a far more provisional character.

In part, this will be because I do not expect to arrive at theological or liturgical statements that will be complete. Beyond me the journey goes on, and I hope simply to participate in a continuing debate.

---

[3]   Liberation theology urges us to see theology as having less a concern with right argument (orthodoxy) than with right action (orthopraxy). Similarly, contemporary liturgy looks beyond the text to the event.

[4]   It was Heidegger who talked of being to death (*Sein zum Tode*), and such a teleological understanding of human life is axiomatic for this book. It is our end rather than our beginning that gives us meaning.

More importantly, I am mindful that what is axiomatic for the quantum physicist holds true beyond the confines of that discipline. At the subatomic level, matter does not exist with certainty at definite places, but rather shows tendencies to exist. Atomic events do not occur with certainty at definite times and in definite ways, but rather show tendencies to occur. As we investigate the nature of matter, we do not find isolated basic building blocks, but a complicated web of relationships between the various parts of the whole. These relationships always include the observer in an essential way so that the classical ideal of an objective description of nature is no longer valid. In atomic physics we can never speak about nature without speaking at the same time about ourselves.

If we were to recast the last two sentences so as to speak of theology rather than physics, we would perhaps discover the extraordinary challenge confronting us. "The classical ideal of an objective description of God is no longer valid. In theology we can never speak about God without speaking at the same time about ourselves." This is not to make of theology an exercise in applied psychology any more than it would be to make atomic physics such an activity. Rather, we may find it inappropriate to rely exclusively on the traditional categories of classical Christian theism as though theology were an exercise external to the theologian.

When we turn later to consider the doctrine of the resurrection of the body, we shall need to address questions of continuity and discontinuity. Similarly, throughout this book I shall want to find continuity and discontinuity with the mainstream of Christian tradition and doctrine. How we manage the balance and shift will reveal our ability to live in the changing philosophical framework of our contemporaries who reject the old ways and affirmations. Hear them we must, if we are to converse with them. Converse with them we must, if we are to reach them. Reach them we must, if we are not to abide alone like the seed that bears no harvest (cf. Jn 12.24). At the same time, if after our dialogue we remain convinced by certain theological expressions of faith, we must be content to give our testimony simply and without arrogance – even if it brings us into contention with colleagues from other disciplines (and from our own!).

This book's principal concern is to show how theological and liturgical studies give meaning and direction to what the Christian Church does when someone dies. Using the methodology of interdisciplinary dialogue, I hope to indicate ways in which liturgists and officiants can remain faithful to the central story of the death and resurrection of Jesus while ministering in the pastoral setting of death and bereavement.

The contemporary shift

For the liturgist who surveys the historical evidence for how death has been marked in the past, there is a variety of sources. Liturgical texts provide an indication of the Church's official practices. Diaries (especially those of parish clergy) show how local variations meet specific instances of death. Public records (including, of course, newspaper reports and in more recent times film and video) add an extra-ecclesiastical dimension. To this last category we may with some caution add that of literature. Novelists, playwrights and poets may for their own purposes exaggerate what they describe, but they work within the context of their own social experience and for that reason provide another commentary which fills out the general picture.

The history of the Western observance of death as we glean it from the public (as opposed to church) record indicates that until comparatively recently, religious (and in particular Christian) practice has predominated. In Europe, with its tradition of state churches, this will not unduly surprise us. In North America, despite the formal separation of church and state, we may imagine that the early European immigrant-settlers brought the practices to which they were accustomed from the societies they were leaving.

Yet by the time of the American War of Independence and the emergence from colonial status, there were other social changes afoot. In Europe the Enlightenment formalised and made respectable scepticism about and opposition to the claims of religion and the Church's easy assumption of political power and overwhelming intellectual control underwritten by spiritual authority. The Industrial Revolution brought with it huge shifts of population from small rural communities where everyone knew everyone else to huge conurbations of relative personal anonymity. The urban parish priest could no longer expect to know every member of his parish, and could no longer control church attendance in the manner of the country parson.

That anonymity and loss of first-hand pastoral contact had huge implications for the conduct of funerals. The service books assumed a local setting in which the priest, the deceased and the mourners were known to one another. The opening rubrics of the funeral service in the 1662 *Book of Common Prayer* run as follows:

> *Here is to be noted, that the Office ensuing is not to be used for any that die unbaptized, or excommunicate, or have laid violent hands upon themselves.*

> *The Priest and Clerks meeting the Corpse at the entrance of the church-yard, and going before it, either into the Church, or towards the Grave, shall say, or sing . . .*

In the urban context with its mobile population the priest still might easily be able to ascertain whether the deceased had committed suicide. However, he might have had rather more difficulty knowing beyond the simple questioning of the mourners whether the deceased had been baptised or excommunicated. The shift from rural and pastoral intimacy to urban and industrial anonymity had vast implications. It is not difficult to see how the complaint, so regularly made in our own time, that funerals are impersonal arises. The busy urban priest who may be asked to conduct a hundred or more funerals a year has little chance of offering the pastoral care which mourners understandably feel to be their right.

In addition, there is an increasing emphasis on personal rights giving rise to an accompanying sense of grievance which, if not met, can only apparently be assuaged by recourse to the legal processes of the courts. The funeral director and the funeral officiant are increasingly seen as purveyors of a professional service with whom the bereaved enter into a contract for the provision of that service. Where mistakes are made, a growing number of mourners are looking for financial redress.

Death and control

Not the least of the changes that has occurred in the management of death has been in the area of control. Death is increasingly understood as involving issues of control.

When death comes, it is frequently construed as a failure or inability of doctors to prolong life. When someone dies in hospital (particularly during or after surgery) we want to know why; and the first people we look at are the doctors. Doctors themselves often collude with this reading of events, and in order to ward off criticism or blame use language that avoids suggestions of control. "We lost Mr Smith on the table," they say. To lose something (or in this case someone) is unfortunate, but all of us from time to time lose something. It is beyond our control, we are not to blame; it just happens.

However, the language of control is not so easily dismissed, especially when it is reinforced by the signs of power and control which we encourage doctors to display: white coats, diplomas on the wall, the consultation which is arranged to the convenience of the clinician rather than that of the patient, the assumption that the hospital is an arena in which there are experts who know and patients who must undergo treatment. All of these indicators propose a competence to which we must submit, and because generally those indicators are justified, we willingly do so. Our co-operation, however, is based on an assumption of care. There is a duty of care, implicit in visiting the doctor, and made explicit when we sign consent forms, which is offended when things go wrong. Often, that offence is not really justified. Those charged with our treatment have done their best, have consulted widely and have exercised diligence and skill. Despite this, the patient dies. On occasion, there have been mistakes that should not have occurred, and at this point lawyers enter and suggest that there should be compensation for what has gone wrong. It is a small step from that understandable reaction to the extreme litigiousness which looks for blame and compensation at every twist and turn. Sometimes, there is nothing to be learned except that death is inevitable. If not at this time, at some time death will come and no doctor or lawyer will stop it.

The excessive preoccupation with control, blame and compensation introduce additional stress in bereavement. Anger is allowed full expression – is even inflated – with consequent difficulties in coming to terms with the finality of death and with the need to move forward. Such a result has implications for the pastoral officiant who may find the preparation of the funeral made considerably more difficult by an all-consuming agenda of "blame and claim" obscuring the Christian proclamation of forgiveness and hope even in death.

The mechanization of death

If the notions of control and blame have implications for the pastoral liturgists, they are not the only shifts in popular attitudes to death that have occurred in recent times. We are right to observe the change in the arena of natural death (from home to hospital) and in its observance (from something open to something hidden), yet the twentieth century saw another aspect of death which has resulted in considerable changes in popular attitudes and observance. That aspect has been mass death. Two World Wars in the first half of the century and subsequent wars of independence and of repression in the second half of the century led to the mass slaughter of combatants and civilians. Many never saw what or who killed them; death became mechanised and remote. Holocausts of ethnic and social groups in Europe and Africa re-enacted Herod's massacre of the innocents. From these horrors came the further horrors of mass memorials, of mass graves, of millions simply missing unburied and unremembered.

To look at the walls of national war memorials with their thousands of names carved into the stone is mind-numbing. We cannot take it all in, and so we focus on a few and let them stand for all. To see in countless small villages and hamlets war memorials where the same family name comes five or six times in the space of a couple of years challenges our sense of normality. The cost to communities is unimaginable.[5] To travel through Northern France and to see one after another graveyards full of the dead still lined with the precision of a military parade for inspection is horrifying. What are the bodies of men from Algeria, Australia, Canada, India, Morocco, New Zealand, Pakistan, the United States and the rest doing here in Picardy, on the Somme?

With the mechanisation of death into a mass-production line came the industrialisation of disposal. Alongside the mass burials came the mass cremations. Death and disposal became numerical and identity was threatened.[6] In our contemporary experience, the disposal of the dead is similarly frequently seen as a production line. This is not always the fault of those who manage our crematoria, but the utilitarian feel of much of the disposal system has led to a revolt. Anonymity is not what mourners require. Increasingly, funeral officiants are asked to celebrate the life of the one who has died and to mark the funeral rites with personal favourites strung together, as it were, like beads on a necklace: poems, pieces of music and eulogies all combine to resist any thought that we are all the same in death.[7] What people ask for is to celebrate the individuality of the deceased.

This emphasis on profound personalisation in death rites marches alongside a decline in belief in eternal life and the resurrection of the dead.[8] Eternal life is now a rosebush and an inscribed name in the crematorium's garden of remembrance.

To acknowledge this is simply to recognise what is happening among us; no more. The question for the Church is how we minister to the shifting attitudes to death and its observance. Do we accept the changes and try to incorporate them in our death rites, or do we resist them? The question is not new to liturgists, for it is the same question

---

[5]   Sedbergh School, in Cumbria, in the North West of England has a vast colonnaded war memorial nearly fifty yards long. It lists former teachers and pupils of the school who died in the two World Wars. Many other schools boast similar memorials. What is terrifying here (as elsewhere) is that the list arises from a school of no more than 400 boys – all of whom were of the "officer class". Most of them would have died before the age of twenty-one. For many their last words would have been, "Follow me, men".

[6]   Of course, in the military graves and at the military memorials an immense effort is taken to ensure that all personal details are properly recorded where they are known. Where details are not known, considerable work is undertaken to discover what can be learnt. At Auschwitz, in the killing fields of Cambodia, in Armenia, in Rwanda, the dead are less fortunate. They are anonymous and those they loved and who loved them have no idea of where they lie.

[7]   The ancient emphasis of Christian funeral rites that in death we are indeed all the same is not congenial to our contemporaries who have been told that they are unique to the exclusion of the recognition that we are all the same.

[8]   Despite the Apostles' and Nicene Creeds, fewer and fewer churchgoers believe in the resurrection of the dead. Many of those who do subscribe to the idea of an afterlife predominantly believe either in reincarnation or in a kind of family reunion in the sky. For all our attempts at demythologising and our descriptions of "man come of age", myth is alive and kicking in popular culture.

posed by inculturation of the liturgy. Pastorally, we always seek to minister to people as they are. Yet we may still be dissatisfied with leaving them where they are. The gospel adapts to some aspects of culture, yet at other points it refuses to be absorbed, to conform.[9] In such a delicate area, the pastoral liturgist has to tread carefully.

The control and mechanisation of the funeral

Perhaps it ought not to surprise us that mourners want to claim control of the funeral. Fewer and fewer families now prepare the bodies of their dead for the funeral. The washing of the body is either done at the hospital or hospice by nursing staff, or by undertakers and funeral directors at their professional premises. Sometimes mourners only arrive to see the body after it has been laid out and dressed in a commercial shroud. By this time it seems too late to ask that those they loved should be dressed in their own clothes. Alternatively, the body may be laid out in some life-like pose as though to deny the reality of what has occurred. The shock of discovering granny sitting up, wearing her spectacles and reading a book, may be grimly humorous or deeply offensive to those who knew that granny was functionally illiterate.[10]

Increasingly families want control, and the one place where they feel they must have that control is at the funeral. So the funeral officiant is presented in varying strength with requests that will make the funeral specific to the one who has died. Against the background of lost control, there is a strong pastoral constraint to accommodate the wishes of the family. A favourite poem, a favourite piece of music, something placed in the coffin (a teddy bear or a bottle of whisky), a tribute by a family member or close friend – such requests are frequently made. Some officiants raise no questions; others have serious reservations. Some encourage this participation; others permit it; yet others refuse it.

The pastoral concern is a powerful factor in the way we decide how to proceed; but, if it is the only consideration, other difficulties may loom. What poetry is appropriate, what music apt? This is not simply a question of "high" and "low" art. Can Swinburne's words, wonderful though they are, be used with integrity at a Christian funeral?

> From too much love of living,
> From hope and fear set free,
> We thank with brief thanksgiving
> Whatever gods may be
> That no man lives for ever,
> That dead men rise up never,
> That even the weariest river
> Winds somewhere safe to sea.

[9] St Paul's missionary activity shows two different approaches in two different situations. At Athens, he engages in inculturation as he adapts his method of proclamation. Among the Galatian Christians he resists the prevailing cultural norm of circumcision and is prepared to pursue the issue at the Council of Jerusalem.

[10] This is an actual instance reported to me by a colleague. The funeral director's professional pride in displaying granny "like she was when she was alive" was never addressed, since the family were lost for words and, not knowing what to say – or how to say it – said nothing.

The sentiment is beautifully expressed, but it is profoundly other than Christian. It is not simply a matter of taste – for some that would rule out half the hymnbook! The question is a theological one, and the prevailing sentiment in the immediate aftermath of death is not necessarily a sufficient cause by itself to accede to every request.

There is a growing pressure for tributes and eulogies to be included in the funeral liturgy. Viewers of the service at Westminster Abbey following the death of Diana, Princess of Wales, saw and remember the powerful oration of her brother over the coffin (they do not remember the prayers), filmgoers remember *Four Weddings and a Funeral*, watchers of the television soap operas see funerals on their screens with characters giving tributes to other characters, and they want the same opportunity. The pastor who permits such addresses is confronted by a number of subsidiary questions. If Auntie Ethel is allowed her say, why should not cousin Jack (who is at daggers drawn with Auntie) be allowed his chance to correct (or further disturb) the record? Where do such tributes come? If they follow the sermon, will they obscure the gospel hope of the resurrection as the wave of sentiment or boisterous good humour engulfs the congregation-become-audience?

Such questions ought not simply to be answered in response to the pressure of the immediate events, even though without them there would be no funeral. Christian liturgy is more than a ritualised farewell to the dead with a few hymns and prayers. At the heart of the Christian observance of funeral rites is the proclamation that the death and resurrection of Jesus change everything. Death is no longer simply an end without hope. Death is the gate to life eternal – not by some wishful thinking, some whistling in the dark, but by the mighty act of God in Christ. The Christian funeral is primarily a remembrance of this person's death set in the framework of the Easter event. It is not our hope that Uncle Fred was on balance a decent enough old chap – a bit of a rogue, but with a heart of gold – whom God will be delighted to have staying in the heavenly Hilton. Our hope is the salvation made possible, not by our human accounting system of good and bad, but by the grace of God manifest in raising Christ from the dead.

When this is the funeral's agenda, the officiant accepts a further set of constraints, and occasionally there is a clash. There is no pain-free solution. To allow all the family requires may obscure the Christ whose death encompasses all human death. To deny the family may equally obscure the Christ who came not for the righteous but for sinners – of whom the Church is, of course, comprised.

It is not the purpose of this book to suggest how these tensions should be creatively held and balanced. I have raised the issue in order to indicate that funerals are never unmixed occasions. The mourners and the Church both have agendas and the officiant has often to negotiate.

The shape of the book

In the next four chapters, I shall reflect on how death is marked in a society which no longer assumes that the Christian Church has a privileged position in shaping and presiding over the rites of death. I shall attempt to listen to those engaged in the life and medical sciences. How do their theoreticians and practitioners understand and respond to death? What are the implications for theology?

I shall then turn to the philosophers, ethicists and lawyers to ask not simply about the nature of death but about its value, its meaning and status. In hearing some of their answers, we will discover other questions for theology.

Lastly, I will examine the findings of those working in the social sciences. In particular, I shall make enquiries of psychologists and anthropologists. From them I hope to learn about the inward experience of death and bereavement, and its ritual expression.

With the issues raised by these disciplines, we shall look in Chapters Six and Seven at how theologians and biblical scholars respond. As well as examining questions about death in general, we shall ask how the death of Jesus defines or shapes our living and our understanding of what it means to be human. In response to questions about the body and the soul, I shall endeavour to offer a theological anthropology of my own.

I shall then narrow the focus to the area of Christology. How does our understanding of what it means to be human affect our understanding of who Jesus was? Does this have any implications for our understanding of the Paschal Mystery – the Easter event – or for the doctrine of the atonement?

When we have come to some sort of theological conclusions, we shall consider some of the historical background to the tradition of Christian funerals (predominantly, but not exclusively) in the Western Church. (A separate and detailed review of liturgical texts will be undertaken in Volume II.)

The final chapter of Volume I will begin with a specific consideration of the rites surrounding the deaths of three very public figures: Diana, Princess of Wales; Basil Hume, Cardinal Archbishop of Westminster; and Queen Elizabeth, the Queen Mother. All three come from the British scene (which is the one that I know best), but each had, to a greater or lesser extent, an international effect. All three liturgical events took place in London churches (two in Westminster Abbey, one in Westminster Cathedral); all three were broadcast on television. There the similarity ends.

Because (as I understand it) all theological statement is partial and provisional, I shall conclude by inviting others to respond. I shall invite revision and correction and I anticipate disagreement and reservation. For some I shall have said far too much. For others I shall have said too little. For yet others, I fear that I shall have spoken in a foreign language. Such is the fate of those who dare to write. The word on the page appears to express something finished or fully formed, when often it marks something provisional and tentative. What follows is intended to be descriptive more than prescriptive. Sometimes, I shall make strong judgements. I hope I shall have evidence to support my assertions. More often, I shall be recording my own uncertainty. For that reason, if for no other, my final words will be to ask for debate and enlightenment.

CHAPTER 2

Ritual Blunder

What are funerals supposed to do?

In 1965 – the very year of Geoffrey Gorer's book on the social semiotics of death and bereavement,[1] the Liturgical Commission of the Church of England offered an answer to this question in its introduction to the Second Series of Alternative Services. It wrote:

> Having faced the question afresh in the light of theological and pastoral considerations, the Commission puts forward the following fivefold answer:
>
> (a)   To secure the reverent disposal of the corpse.
>
> (b)   To commend the deceased to the care of our heavenly Father.
>
> (c)   To proclaim the glory of our risen life in Christ here and hereafter.
>
> (d)   To remind us of the awful certainty of our own coming death and judgement.
>
> (e)   To make plain the eternal unity of Christian people, living and departed, in the risen and ascended Christ.
>
> It would perhaps be natural to add a sixth point, namely the consolation of the mourners; but the Commission believes that this object should be attained by means of the objects already included in its answer.[2]

It is worth noting that the primary emphasis is upon dealing with the dead. One of the concerns of this book is to answer the question, "Who is the funeral for?" and to suggest that funerary rites have to address both the living and the dead. Frequently, the emphasis is placed more strongly on the pastoral care of the bereaved, and the idea of the rite effecting anything for the dead is obscured or denied. For the present, I wish simply to note that for the Anglican Communion the difficulty is particularly sharp and that the Liturgical Commission's statement was an attempt to address the issue.

An example of this difficulty is found in the Church of England where the Catholic and the Evangelic streams do not always sit together easily, and where debate about what can be done for the dead is ever present. Non-Catholics will find difficulty with those who suggest that the liturgy can in any way have an ontological effect on the dead. For those who belong to the Protestant traditions, prayers for the dead are highly problematical. Although such prayers had been reintroduced in the 1928 rites, that revision had not gained final authorization.[3] The 1928 rite could be understood as an option for the Catholic wing of the Church of England in a way that the *Alternative Service Book 1980* never could be. Michael Perham described the result in Series Three

---

[1]   Gorer, G. 1965. *Death, Grief and Mourning in Contemporary Britain* (London: Cresset). See below, Chapter Five.

[2]   *Alternative Services. Second Series.* 1965. (London: The Church of England Liturgical Commission: 105-106).

[3]   The 1928 book was approved by the Church of England, but failed to gain Parliamentary assent.

as "the sort of tinkering required to modernize the language and reach an acceptable compromise on prayer for the dead".[4]

Although the problems are particularly acute for the Anglican traditions, their debate is one which the whole Church has to address. In the funeral rite what are we doing for the dead? If there were no corpse, there would be no funeral, and the bereaved would need no rite of passage. Their passage is secondary and contingent upon the primary and necessary rite for the dead. Knox's solution of ignoring the dead (except for the public health requirement of burial) and addressing the service, or rather the sermon, exclusively to the living is not a good solution if the rite's primary focus is on the dead.[5]

The Liturgical Commission concluded that the funeral is also an occasion of ministry to the living, to the bereaved. This conclusion is universally accepted; and we might be forgiven for thinking that there is no further problem. However, what we and those who mourn believe about death and the dead will determine how we minister to the bereaved, and on these matters (as I have already suggested) there is a divergence of opinion. Moreover, I am eager to resist the widely accepted notion that the aim of ministry to the bereaved is to "get them back to normal". I shall address the work of psychiatrists and grief counsellors, and review the implications of what their studies show for the work of Christian ministry in Chapter Five.

At the heart of the Liturgical Commission's statement is an affirmation about our sharing in the resurrection life of Christ. The Commission intended this as an allusion to the communion of saints; but it also reminds us, however obliquely, of the social nature of death at the human level. Death is not simply a private event; there is a social dimension. At its most earthbound, there are certificates to be completed and legalities to be observed; but beyond these duties, there is the sense of inter-relatedness which John Donne articulates in his celebrated seventeenth meditation.[6]

Social anthropology also makes a contribution to the agenda. If the social life of a human being is remembered at all in the funeral, it is usually in the homily. I shall want to consider whether liturgy can better articulate the social nature of death than by assuming that a gathering of mourners or a few words about the deceased's family, working life and leisure pursuits is an adequate expression in itself.[7]

The underlying question is, "What is the pastoral agenda when we attempt to address these individuals and groups in our liturgies?" Other questions follow. Is the Christian funeral simply an expression of practical, kindly care – and no more? If so,

---

[4]   Perham, M. 1989. "The Funeral Liturgy", in Perham, M. (ed.), *Towards Liturgy 2000* (London. SPCK/Alcuin Club: 53)

[5]   Calvin argued that burial was important as a sign of the resurrection (*The Institutes of the Christian Religion*, III.xxv.5 and 8). John Knox's Genevan Service Book of 1556, urged a reverent burial and at the church a "comfortable exhortation to the people" about death and resurrection.

[6]   "No man is an Island, entire of it self; every man is a piece of the Continent, a part of the main; if a clod be washed away by the sea, Europe is the less, as well as if a promontory were, as well as if a manor of thy friends or of thine own were; any man's death diminishes me, because I am involved in Mankind; And therefore never send to know for whom the bell tolls; It tolls for thee". J. Donne, *Devotions upon Emergent Occasions*, Meditation XVII.

[7]   Often the social nature of a particular death is better expressed outside the funeral rite, and particularly in the social gathering which follows the funeral.

how does it differ from a humanist rite? In anthropological terms, can a rite of passage be reduced to a formalised cheerio?

If there is more to the Christian funeral than expressions of sympathy and the recounting of memories, the liturgist needs to be aware of what it is. The Christian funeral is more than just an occasion for human kindness; it is also an arena of confrontation and disclosure. In this arena the ultimate mystery of God is perilously encountered; here the story of God in Christ and the story of this dead person are interwoven. The death of Christ is representative of our death, and the grief of the Father in the death of Jesus is a kerygmatic word to all who mourn.[8] This raises key questions for the Christian funeral: "How does God in Christ relate to the dead and to the living?", and "How does God hold the keys of life and death?" In an attempt to answer, I shall consider how the Paschal Mystery forms the basis of funeral rites. This has been a principal concern of those who have prepared the *Order of Christian Funerals*. Their work has been a response to the sense that death must be answered by resurrection. However, it has perhaps not taken account of what anthropologists call the transitional, or liminal, where chaos threatens to overwhelm order. In the language of the Paschal Mystery this requires that we give detailed attention to Holy Saturday and the descent to the dead. Here is the pivot of the Easter event, and a dynamic myth for the dead and the bereaved in the funeral liturgy.

The gap between expectation and performance

There are four areas in which contemporary funerals are commonly subject to criticism:

–   the officiant's performance may be seen as automatic or in some way uncaring;

–   the liturgical content of some rites may not be always conducive to a helpful rite of passage;

–   the theological presuppositions of rites may not correspond with the beliefs and understandings of those who mourn;

–   the necessary sense of community upon which rites of passage depend for their successful performance may not exist in the course of any particular funeral.

Initially, I shall consider the first two issues; I shall then illustrate how they have impinged upon a particular funeral. I shall then return to consider the final two matters.

Ministerial performance

My own observation of those who officiate at funerals is that the overwhelming majority of ministers want to help those who mourn. Where there is no previous knowledge of the deceased or of the mourners, the way in which ministers set out to achieve their aim is by attempting to create what they hope will be a caring ambience.

---

[8]   This is part of Moltmann's great contribution to the debate.

Many believe that this is produced by careful attention to tone and style. Body gestures and voice timbres are pitched almost in imitation of the doctor's bedside manner.[9] Where there is a good previous connection with the family, the artificiality in which style and tone predominate is diminished. In such cases pastoral care has already been established, and what occurs in the funeral rites is simply part of an existing continuum of ministry.

Frequently, however, the officiant's first knowledge of the death and first meeting with the bereaved is as a result of a funeral director's phone call. Where ministers are able to arrange a meeting with the contact provided by the funeral director – and this is not always the next of kin – the visit which follows may reveal a host of constraints upon what ministers feel themselves able to do at the funeral. Christian funeral rites frequently presume the Christian faith not only of the deceased but also of the mourners. Sometimes the presumption is implicit in the liturgy, on other occasions explicit comment is made in rubrics or other instructions.[10] However, the minister will often find either a faith which was only ever voiced at baptism many years previously or no faith at all. In such circumstances (s)he is placed in a difficult situation: the liturgical forms are Christian, but those for whom they are now being used have no faith at all in the sense which the liturgy assumes. What is required in the minds of many such mourners is much more like a humanist event – a dignified farewell without institutional religious expression.[11] Where there is a serious objection to religious content, the minister may wish to withdraw. But time is often short, and where no alternative officiant can be found, the minister may feel obliged to offer some sort of ritual care for reasons of simple humanity. In such cases, the result may well be unsatisfactory either to the minister, or to the family, or to both.

On other occasions, the officiant may be serving as the duty minister at the crematorium. Here the chance of meeting with the family and planning anything together is fairly remote, and it is very likely that even the most capable minister will be unable to offer anything much more than a standard form with one or two amendments to fit the name of the deceased. It is clear how this kind of situation may leave the mourners feeling cheated – the minister probably has the same reaction.[12]

---

[9] One minister, now himself dead, but in life the possessor of a splendid *basso profundo* voice, was described to me by a colleague as having "a grand graveside manner"!

[10] For example, the *Order of Christian Funerals*, 1990, confidently begins paragraph 4 of its General Introduction: "At the death of a Christian, whose life of faith was begun in baptism and strengthened at the eucharistic table . . ." The first rubric of the Funeral Service in the 1662 *Book of Common Prayer* states: "Here is to be noted, that the Office ensuing is not to be used for any that die unbaptised, or excommunicate, or have laid violent hands upon themselves."

[11] Humanist officiants are available, but funeral directors do not always know whom to contact, and families do not always know how to ask. The British Humanist Association offers help in its publication: Willson, J. W. 1989. *Funerals without God: A Practical Guide to Non-religious Funerals* (London: British Humanist Association). See also, *Civil Funerals:Training Manual* (Huntingdon: Civil Ceremonies Limited, 2002).

[12] In a diary column in *The Independent on Sunday*, dated 21 November 1993, Geraldine Bedell wrote of her recent experience. She began: "The modern municipal funeral can seem a bleak and perfunctory affair. My grandmother had hers last week, and I spent most of the service worrying that the vicar would get her mixed up with someone else. In the event, he did get her name and most of the details right. But it

The sociologist, Tony Walter, proposes that ministers should spend time with families planning the funeral, encouraging them to take the initiative in making the arrangements rather than leaving it to the professionals – ministers or funeral directors.[13] In principle, this is good, but it presupposes a number of things which in practice may not be possible. It assumes that the minister can meet with the family frequently enough, or for long enough, to make such arrangements. At least two things may hinder this. The time may not be available either to the minister or to the family, and the family may not be available in a sufficiently representative form to make the sort of decisions which Walter advocates. Even if the minister and the family meet together, not all families are ready or able in the days immediately following death to make the kind of complex choices which planning a funeral ritual entails. Many non-churchgoers know only a few hymns, of which two are usually "The Lord's my Shepherd" and "Abide with me". Of course, both of these hymns are quite acceptable for use at funerals. But once this choice has been made, the idea of sitting in a group discussing with a stranger what the deceased would have wanted or what they prefer is alien to the majority of people, who are numbed by what has just occurred, and who may well find that the dynamics and atmosphere of such a group do not liberate them at all.

The explanations I have offered so far avoid what is sometimes at the root of the problem: ministerial slackness. It is undeniable that not all funerals receive from ministers the kind of care which mourners have a right to expect: the wrong name is used for the deceased; the prayers are gabbled; the homily either makes so little mention of the deceased that it is clear that no preparation in this area has been made, or the minister describes someone so devoid of faults or weakness that "canonisation precedes interment". Where this sort of incompetence occurs, a serious damage is done.[14]

For many people the pastoral offices are their only experience of church; they have discarded Christian faith and practice as boring, out of touch, and irrelevant. The officiating minister who allows mourners to depart with these opinions hardened has missed an opportunity to put matters right; proclamation becomes ever more difficult.[15]

---

must have been much easier when vicars knew the people they were burying, and did actually bury them, while the relatives threw earth at their coffins and said their sad goodbyes". She concluded: "Vicars ought to encourage people to write or say something themselves, to choose a poem or something else which has mattered to the dead. Otherwise it's hard to feel that the ritual isn't vaguely absurd."

[13] J. A. Walter. 1990. *Funerals – And How To Improve Them* (London: Hodder and Stoughton). Walter argues that the designation "funeral director" indicates a shift in status and role from the old "undertaker", a shift in which the mourners lose control of the funeral.

[14] The Superintendent of a cemetery and crematorium in Manor Park, London, addressing a conference of The Churches' Group on Funerals in Cemeteries and Crematoria, in October 1993, added other horrors: ministers who didn't clip their notes together, so that a sudden gust of wind distributed pieces of paper around the cemetery; ministers who didn't bother to acquaint themselves with the buttons at the crematorium lectern and started the coffin on its journey instead of fading out the taped music; ministers who wouldn't accept the time limitations and caused funerals that followed theirs to have to queue; ministers who forgot – either where the funeral was, or that there was a funeral at all – and failed to turn up. The examples he gave seemed endless; and although he delivered his address with gentleness and humour, the catalogue of disaster was a shameful reproach.

[15] I am not suggesting that the funeral should have a hidden agenda of trying to fill next Sunday's pews with today's bereaved; but the preaching of the gospel is one of the tasks of the Christian Church, and experiences which harden attitudes do not assist the proclamation of the God of life and love.

Liturgical content

The remoteness of much of the Christian faith to contemporary people ought to challenge liturgists and pastoral officiants to be particularly sensitive to the language and ideas in which pastoral liturgy seeks to express itself. A funeral service is not always an unequivocally good example of user-friendliness. Much of what is said must sound strange – even alien – to those who hear it.

Frequently the first words which are spoken are the sentences of scripture as the coffin is borne into the crematorium chapel.

> I am the resurrection and the life, says the Lord; he who believes in me, though he die,
> yet shall he live, and whoever lives and believes in me shall never die.[16]

If the deceased person was indeed a member of a Christian tradition, those who hear these words are entitled to wonder why their relative or friend is dead. Yet beyond the awkwardness of the apparent equation between belief and not dying, there lie the difficulties of using male pronouns when the deceased is female, and of using such a text where no Christian belief was expressed by the deceased in life.

Similarly, in a burial as the coffin is being lowered, these words are heard at the graveside:

> To the One who is able to keep you from falling, . . .[17]

When asked about the appropriateness of such texts, ministers suggest that people know what is meant and that they understand that such words are not to be taken literally. It is uncertain to me that this can be universally assumed. Some mourners are acutely sensitive to the least infelicity of expression, and one detail may colour their recollection and, indeed, the effectiveness of the entirety. Tony Walter argues that mourners "are often in great pain and are unable to take in every word, or even one word". He suggests that it is the general tone which counts, "the ring of language that sounds significant". While I accept the broad thrust of what he says, my own pastoral experience indicates that people do remember oddities, and that often the general impression retained is the result of a particularity which provides a hermeneutic for the whole. The main concern of Walter's argument at this point is for specific, personal and poetic language rather than "stodgy abstract prose" (1990: 227-228), and with this I am in total agreement. Language is important. If Christian liturgy is adequately to meet the occasion of the funeral, it will have to use language which expresses the nature of the relationship between God and the one who has died. For this it will need to address the particular as well as the universal.

---

[16] However, in the rites provided in the service book used in most cemeteries and crematoria, *Funeral Services of the Christian Churches in England* (Canterbury Press, 2000), only the Church of England's order begins with Jn 11.25, 26. The service forms provided from the *Order of Christian Funerals* and from the ecumenical Joint Liturgical Group do not use that particular text.

[17] *Revised Funerals 1987*, General Synod of the Episcopal Church of Scotland, Edinburgh.
A different reading of the same text is proposed by the Church of England's *Alternative Service Book 1980*.

Yet beyond the language of liturgy there is the ritual structure and form which that language expresses.

A case of ritual blunder

For most people the funeral is an experience out of the ordinary. Even for regular churchgoers, the funeral may bring some unfamiliarity. The particularity of the death which confronts the congregation also raises questions with which, for most of the time, people do not concern themselves. Issues of mortality present themselves with an immediacy and urgency which are outside our everyday patterns of thought. The funeral takes us out of the normal routine of life and ritualises not only our fear of death but our grief for this death.

Much of human grief and fear is by its nature inarticulate. Gesture, symbol and music may offer to mourners other ways in which their concerns may be expressed. But as is the case with language, these additional ritual expressions must be carefully prepared. Where the signal is confused, the ritual expression will be ineffective. In his account of the death of his father,[18] Blake Morrison shows how lack of proper preparation causes a sudden lurch in the proceedings. He describes the crematorium committal which followed the church service at his father's funeral:

> It is a short service: two minutes of Albinoni on tape (his Adagio in G minor, a piece I'd taken to playing with doomy repetitiveness just before my father's illness), then the tape fading for three minutes of the vicar. As he speaks of committing to God this beloved servant, he reaches for the rope-pull which will switch the curtains round the coffin and activate the conveyor belt – at which point Malcolm leaps from the front stalls and whisperingly intervenes: the family wish the coffin to remain visible and in place until after the service; it is they who will disappear, not the deceased. The vicar nods, the service ends, Albinoni resumes. . . (Morrison: 198)

Morrison's experience is a negative one for the Church. He is not a churchgoer himself, and so the vicar (a newcomer) starts at a disadvantage:

> The vicar begins to talk – knowledgeably: you wouldn't guess he didn't know my father . . . (Morrison: 195).

The Funeral Director has a name (Malcolm); the vicar has none. The incident at the crematorium chapel is not necessarily the vicar's fault; Malcolm may have forgotten to advise the vicar of the family's wishes, but Morrison is left with a sense of ritual blunder. His prior suppositions about the Church have hardened.

The music was right, but the curtain was wrong; and it is the curtain which is so important. The crematorium curtain may carry for the mourner an unconscious theatrical undertone; as the curtain closes, it marks the end of the play. But in this funeral of a West Yorkshire General Practitioner, the family wants to leave the stage to the central player, the dead man. Whether or not such a decision is symptomatic of a

---

[18]　　Morrison, B, 1993. *And when did you last see your father?* (London: Granta).

refusal to accept the fact of death is irrelevant;[19] the ritual which the family wanted to enact was endangered by an inappropriate gesture.

Whilst this is a specific instance of ritual disorder which is reported by an unusually articulate and observant mourner (Morrison is a journalist and author), it indicates that cultural linkages need to be made for the successful performance of ritual. In the case of the Christian funeral, the liturgy starts with assumptions which the vast majority of mourners does not share. It is to this area of belief that I now wish to turn.

Theological framework

Christian belief lives with the scandal of particularity. Where others may speak of God in nature and in history, Christians affirm that God is revealed primarily and uniquely in the history of Jesus. Yet more, God is present and active most clearly in Jesus the Crucified.[20]

Whilst the death of Jesus may be understood as an example to us of the love which is self-giving to the end, it is unsatisfactory to the major strands of Christian belief to limit the cross simply to an exhortative example. Christian tradition has wanted to explain the death of Jesus as having an atoning power. Saint Paul described the preaching of the cross as a scandal – especially to those who otherwise understood God as entering human history.[21]

What is often construed as an exclusivity continues to be offensive to many, and yet the death of Jesus is an utterly fundamental constituent of the liturgy of Christian funerals. I shall want to argue in Chapters Five and Six that the particularity of Jesus' death is not necessarily exclusive, but is rather a signpost to a universality. Nonetheless, there is an awkwardness here for the conceptual framework of the majority of our contemporaries. I am uncertain whether this difficulty can be resolved without a considerable adjustment either in Christian theology or in contemporary pluralism or in both as they address each other.[22]

A second area of difficulty is that of eschatology both personal and cosmic. The questions "What will happen to me when I die?" and "What will happen at the end of the world?" depend for their answers upon theories of the nature of the human and of the universe.

The Christian Churches have for most of their history held to an anthropology which has distinguished between body and soul (with the frequent division of the soul into mind and spirit). Recent debate has addressed the question of how authentic the body-

---

[19] Throughout the book Morrison describes his emotional ambivalence, but he is far from denying what has happened. The question which forms the title of the book is one that Morrison addresses to the relationship of personality and bodily collapse.

[20] The crucifixion of Jesus is but one act in the drama of the Paschal Mystery and is not to be separated from the whole. I shall be discussing this in Chapter Seven.

[21] 1 Cor 1.23; Gal 5.11. Cf. Rom 9.32; 11.11.

[22] The difficulty for some Christian theology will be in accommodating a wider application of the implications of the death of Christ for the cosmos. For contemporary pluralism, the difficulty will be in accepting the continued emphasis of Jesus as the focus of universal history.

soul anthropology is.[23] The suggestion has been urged by some that the body-soul anthropology was alien to the Old Testament, and that the earliest Christian preaching talked of the resurrection of the body as opposed to the immortality of the soul. What we believe about death has consequences for the way in which we mark its advent by liturgies, and that belief in life after death is less widely embraced than Christian funeral rites assume.

Part of the modern disenchantment with the language of Christian discourse as it addresses individual eschatology is concerned with the resurrection of the body. Two difficulties present themselves. Firstly, there is a general perception that "science" has in some way demonstrated that we do not possess souls, that there is a high degree of improbability amounting to impossibility that the body which has dissolved – either in the ground, the fire, or the sea – can be reconstituted as the body it once was. This for many people leads them to the conclusion that personal survival beyond death and (more certainly) the resurrection of the body are not believable.[24] Secondly, the narrowness of concern with individual survival, given the ecological and military threats to the planet, seems to others to betray an exaggerated egoism.

If the concept of life after death is no longer an article which Christian faith can assume, then belief in the final judgement and heaven and hell is even more contentious.[25] Despite the frequent popular formulation of the problem of evil with its underlying call for God to do justice, any theodicy which proposes a *post mortem* delay is impatiently dismissed. Theologies which talk of judgement in terms of God putting things right or of God being in process have not yet been able to root themselves in public awareness; and those, who in sympathy with popular questions about God and the creation have tried to speak of God in other ways, have been derided in the media. There is nothing new in this, but it does serve to illustrate the gulf between the language of theological discourse and popular belief. In the funeral, when the Christian Church seeks to minister to the bereaved, this gulf can quickly become a credibility gap.

Some Christian theologians have suggested that after the horrors of global war, language about heaven and hell can no longer be used. Certainly, glib talk is no help – but it never has been. However, if theologians disengage from talk about hell, not everyone else has felt so fastidious. Novelists and dramatists have investigated the theme with an urgency born of the very events which silence others. Film-makers have portrayed the violence which darkens the human psyche; and titles like *Apocalypse Now*, *The Omen*, and *The Exorcist* join the existentialist enquiry into what is seen as the meaninglessness of so much of human life. Among the plays, *Waiting for Godot* is a

[23] See, for example, Pannenberg, W. 1985. *Anthropology in Theological Perspective* (Edinburgh: T. & T. Clark) and Tugwell, S. 1009. *Human Immortality and the Redemption of Death* (London: Darton, Longman and Todd).

[24] I think that this is a fair summary of the popular understanding of "science". I do not think that it is a fair summary of the conclusions of natural scientists, who are as divided about life after death as are the generality of people. Further, it begs the question as to whether absence of proof is the same as proof of absence. Even given the majority's scepticism about life after death, there is a wide interest in the paranormal, in near-death experiences, in the occult, or anything which suggests that "we are not alone".

[25] Various surveys in recent years reveal that increasing numbers of churchgoers do not believe in life after death.

waiting for deliverance; *Huis Clos* is set in a hell which initially seems unthreatening but grows darker and darker until the realisation comes: *l'enfer, c'est les autres*. There is no need for brimstone, stake or gridiron; hell is other people.[26] Nonetheless, all three occupants of the room are dead! Sartre, for all his existentialism, still places hell beyond death.

The funeral liturgist requires enormous courage in facing these themes: in articulating the darkness of death, and in expressing the Christian hope. It cannot be done in essays; Tony Walter is right to contrast the lifelessness of prose with the energy of poetry. Where the Christian faith is proclaiming life in the midst of death, it must address the heart with imaginative fire.

Ritual community

An additional concern of Chapter Five will be a consideration of the theory of rites of passage. At least one of the preconditions for ritual coherence is the existence of a community with common understandings and traditions about what life and death are, about what values we may attach to life and death, and about what the rite is.

One does not have to subscribe to the view that there is no such thing as society, to observe that a vibrant sense of community is much diminished in contemporary living. In part this is a result of increased personal mobility. It is not simply that people move from the area in which they grew up when they reach adulthood, there is a greater movement in the search for work. Fewer people hold one job for all their working lives. More people live in one town and travel to another for work, and to yet another for shopping or recreation. Increasingly families are becoming scattered, and the nuclear family can no longer automatically look to extended family support within a few minutes' walk. This geographical dislocation means that sometimes families are only found all together at weddings and funerals. In such circumstances, there will be little sense of community even within the family.

Perhaps this might matter less if people were able to make communities where they live. However, where workers are commuting to large conurbations, leaving home early and returning home late, the occasions for shared life are fewer. Even in rural Britain, in the villages, there is no guarantee of a sense of community – especially where villages have become the homes of rich city-dwellers seeking the rural idyll.[27] Early twenty-first century Britain is in huge social flux, and the resultant patterns of shift weaken the social groupings which normally foster the common history, identity, customs, language, and memory which give shape and meaning to social ritual.[28]

---

[26] Sartre, Jean-Paul. *Huis Clos*, scene 5.

[27] Two examples of the urbanite disruption of village life will show what I mean. A farmer in the Home Counties found people moving into the village protesting about the smell of his pigs, and using planning regulations to force him out of business. A North Yorkshire jobbing builder was told by newcomers that his business was destroying the peace of the countryside; his retort was that the countryside was made by people working, not by people coming home to watch their television. In both instances, heavy pressure was brought to bear on local people by those whose common cause was privacy.

[28] Richard Sennett (1986) argues in the opening chapter of *The Fall of Public Man* (London: Faber and Faber) that there has been a substantial shift in the nature of what it means to be public and to be private

Alongside the geographical scattering, there has been a gradual dissolution of the community of faith. Religious belief has largely been privatised, and those religious communities who seek to bind themselves together under a clear and close identity are frequently treated with suspicion. Their determination not to lose their identity is variously seen as a refusal to inculturate (that is, here, to become "British"), as a ghetto instinct, or as religious fundamentalism.[29] The privatisation of belief has led to two distinct challenges to ritual community. It is no longer possible to assume that there is a consensus about what may be believed – or even about what may be disbelieved. It is quickly becoming an *a priori* assumption that religion deals with the individual's private beliefs rather than addressing public issues. When what the individual believes is her/his own business anyway, and when the expression of wider moral challenge to public policy is seen as trespass, the challenge to traditional Christian concepts of community is very deep.

These are issues to which the liturgist and the officiant must be sensitive. It is not that they can change the sociological groundswell by telling the sea to turn back in their rites and ceremonies, but choices will have to be made about how community can be fostered so that ritual can be effective. Two possibilities seem immediately available; and although I present them here as alternatives, they may in fact be developed together. Either the officiant attempts to generate an *ad hoc* community (largely, I think, the present practice), or the attempt can be made to produce a liturgical community along the lines proposed in the *Order of Christian Funerals*, in which the local congregation becomes a community of consolation.[30]

Conclusion

Can the pastoral and theological agenda which I have outlined be expressed in liturgy alone? I shall suggest that, while a rich variety of liturgical provision is a vital part of the process by which the living express their new relationship with the dead, a rite of passage serves to formalise in communal language a process which requires other complementary forms of ministry and human care. Ultimately the rite cannot perform what the community does not share.

However dazzling our liturgies, they are dust; they require breath to bring them to life. The words of Jesus to pious and holy men, religious leaders struggling with their scriptures to interpret and be obedient to their understanding of God, may be relevant here:

---

and that the nineteenth-century crisis of public life led to obsession with selfhood and private space. The nature of common life has changed.

[29] Residential zoning has long been a feature of British life; and those who are loud in their condemnation of "Little Pakistan" in some of the old East Lancashire cotton towns are frequently complacent about the quiet avenues of detached houses that exist in "desirable residential areas" of the very same towns. The latter are just as much ghettos as the former in housing terms, but my own observation is that ritual awareness is far higher in "Little Pakistan".

[30] *Order of Christian Funerals*, "General Introduction", paragraphs 9ff.

You pore over the writings, because you think that in them you have the life of the age to come; and they give their witness to me, but you do not come to me to gain life.[31]

To summarise, death alerts us to questions of anthropology, of psychiatry, of the natural and biological sciences, of law and ethics, of theology, Christology and eschatology. Funerals address these issues more or less directly, and the Christian liturgist and officiant are given the task of particularising the universal when confronted by the death of a human.

---

[31] Jn 5.39, 40 – my translation. Later in the Fourth Gospel, Jesus contrasts the spirit which gives life and the flesh which has nothing to offer (6.63).

CHAPTER 3

Medicine and the Law

What is death? The medical definition: failure and limitation

The starting point for many Christian theologians in considering human death has been the story of the Fall, and the primary focus of discussions that have begun in this way has been an aetiological one. When the question is asked, "What is death?", the answer has been "God's punishment for sin". Those who make this reply stand in a strong theological tradition and can claim among their champions the apostle Paul with his declaration that the wages of sin is death (Rom 6.23). Yet Paul's affirmation is not really an answer to the question "What is death?" so much as to the question "Why do we die?"

On the whole, the question "What is death?" does not seem to have troubled theologians in quite the same way as the question about why we die. Inasmuch as there has been concern, it has been rather more with what happens after death than what death itself is. By ignoring the question of what death is, we allow what may appear to be otherwise no more than speculation to proceed in detachment from much of the work of anthropologists, medical scientists, philosophers and jurists. Such a detachment means that Christian theologians make a less significant contribution to the ethical and pastoral debates about death than they should do.

The question "What happens to me when I die?" may receive a variety of responses, but for contemporary understanding the medical answer is almost certainly the one which will gain the widest acceptance.[1]

Death arrives clinically by one of two major routes:

- failure of the heart and lungs leading to failure in the brain;
- severe damage in the brainstem leading to failure in the brain and subsequently to failure of the heart and lungs.[2]

The first of these is the more common process. The brain ceases to function as the vital supplies of oxygen carried in the bloodstream come to a halt with the failure of the heart and lungs. This can happen gradually as entropy and increasing age conspire; or it may occur traumatically by a heart attack or by catastrophic loss of blood resulting from major injury sustained in, for example, a road accident or a wounding (whether criminal or surgical).

---

[1] Any medical definition of death is provisional. In part it is dependent upon the advances in medical science, in part upon the agreement of those who set the legal and ethical boundaries. The legal and philosophical debates are introduced in this chapter, and a detailed discussion of the jurisprudence relating to the persistent vegetative state (PVS) is undertaken in the following chapter.

[2] A detailed discussion of the process of death is available in Nuland, S. B. 1994. *How We Die* (London: Chatto and Windus). It is an explicit, and at times discouraging, account of the clinical process of dying.

In the case of brainstem fatality, there follows a deterioration of the control systems governing the heart, lungs and cardiovascular system. This in turn produces a chaotic breakdown in the control processes for the heart and lungs. Death follows. In such circumstances, the heart and lungs may be mechanically ventilated, but when this support is withdrawn breathing and circulation will inevitably cease – usually fairly rapidly.[3]

In 1976, British medical authorities issued a statement giving advice on ways of diagnosing brain death.[4] Their advice was extremely detailed, but began describing three coexisting conditions which were indispensable for considering such a diagnosis:

–   the patient had to be deeply comatose;

–   the patient had to be maintained on a ventilator because spontaneous respiration had previously become inadequate or had ceased altogether;

–   there was to be no doubt that the patient's condition was due to irremediable structural brain damage, and a diagnosis of the disorder which could lead to brain death should have already been fully established.

A series of diagnostic tests was described by which the three conditions might be confirmed. Doctors were reminded that tests should be repeated in order to eliminate observer error, and further observations were added for the guidance of practitioners – whether more or less experienced.

When we consider death in purely medical terms, we may speak of it as the irretrievable breakdown of those processes which require energy and oxygen and of those systems which maintain homeostasis between anabolism and catabolism. Death is a process as well as an event, and the descent into chaos occurs both before the person is pronounced dead and after that moment.[5]

To offer such a precise clinical definition as an answer to the question "What happens when I die?" in a pastoral context would be profoundly insensitive and shocking. The analytical guidelines which are offered to organ transplant teams confront us in the starkest terms with our mortality. Most people are like the British clown and comedian, Spike Milligan, who said: "Dying does not frighten me; I just don't want to be there when it happens."[6]

Shorn of its modern use of sophisticated diagnostic techniques and hardware, anyone throughout human history would recognise what is being described. It is that

---

[3]   There are extraordinary circumstances where after brainstem death residual electrical impulses in the heart may be measured by electrocardiograph, for example after execution in the electric chair, for periods as long as 30 minutes. Normally events move very much more quickly.

[4]   "Diagnosis of Brain Death" (*British Medical Journal*, 13 November 1976: 1187-1188). The guidance was primarily offered to organ transplant teams working in hospitals. Surgeons, wishing to obtain organs for transplant in as good a state as possible, wanted to remove donor organs at the earliest opportunity. In order to allay suspicion, and to protect doctors from any suggestion that they were acting improperly in what would inevitably be emotional circumstances, the advice was issued with detailed guidelines by which death could be properly and incontrovertibly diagnosed.

[5]   A later chapter will address this understanding of death as chaos, and will undertake a theological review of personal anthropology.

[6]   Mr Milligan died in 2002. The remark has also been attributed to the American film director and actor, Woody Allen.

process during which life and breath leave the body, and the person becomes a corpse. Whether we hold a bronze mirror to the nose, or pass the final stitch of the seaman's canvas shroud through the same sensitive member,[7] the absence of breath from the nostril and the stilling of the pulse indicate to us the advent of death.

For many of our contemporaries, death is defined in terms of medical failure or limitation. People die, it is believed, because the doctors cannot keep them alive. As medical science and technology advance, the physiological and neurological functions which stimulate and sustain life can be maintained where otherwise they would fail and the patient die. Switching off support systems produces a very sharp division between life and death in the popular imagination, and where doctors take the decision no longer to use extraneous mechanical support there is inevitably an acknowledgement of limitation.[8]

When we describe death in these terms, we are using the language of control. To exercise control in any given situation or process, there must be an elimination of as many random elements as possible. In the control of death this means the prevention of disease and sepsis, and a high degree of precaution against accidental or deliberate injury. Hospitals are designed to offer an environment in which these aims may be achieved; consequently, much of our care of those near death occurs in hospitals. Inevitably (if ironically), hospitals have become the commonest place of death.

The arena of death: home and hospital

Not the least of the changes which has occurred in the management of death has been in the area of control. Philippe Ariès' important contributions to the anthropology of death (Ariès, 1974 and 1987) have included an historical survey of Western attitudes to death in which he has described the transfer of control of the dying process. He argues that whereas in the Middle Ages control was held by the dying person or her/his family and was most likely to occur at home or in the community to which (s)he belonged, the predominant place for death in the modern age is in the hospital where control is held by the medical profession.[9]

---

[7] The final stitch through the nose was an 18th and 19th century custom in Royal Navy to detect those who were shamming death in battle. It was, apparently, one of the few diagnostic devices believed never to have failed!

[8] I am not convinced that we ought to talk of "failure" in the circumstances. Failure is frequently accompanied by feelings of guilt, and in talking of failure we induce guilt in those described as having failed. Where the limits of knowledge and care have been reached, then incrimination is worse than useless – it is counter-productive.

[9] Ariès, P. 1974. *Western Attitudes towards Death* (Baltimore: Johns Hopkins University Press) and 1987. *The Hour of Our Death* (London: Penguin Books, reprinted). In the opening chapter of *Western Attitudes towards Death*, Ariès argues that in the millennium before the early modern period the descriptions of death that we possess show a number of common phenomena: awareness in the dying that death was near, preparation made by the dying for death – consisting of prescribed ritual postures and gestures, and a number of formalised remembrances and pardonings articulated in the presence of the communities to which they belonged. However, some of the source documents which Ariès quotes present the twenty-first century reader with evidential problems. For example, *La mort d'Artus*, *Les enfances de Lancelot du Lac*, *La chanson de Roland*, *Le roman de Tristan et Iseult*, a hagiographical account of Saint Martin of Tours and *Don Quixote* are all accounts which we may suspect of containing some elements of

Ariès draws the disturbing conclusion that the support, which in the medieval period had come from the family and community who surrounded the dying person, is no longer available; death is isolated. Whatever our misgivings about Ariès' observations on death in the medieval period, it is worth noting that in 1985 26% of deaths in England and Wales occurred in the person's own home, while 69% occurred in institutions.[10]

Toward the end of Chapter Five, we shall consider how this change in the arena of death may have consequences for the ritual community at a funeral.[11] For the present, we may note that there appears to have been a shift in the control of death from the one who is dying and her/his family and friends to medical advisers whose concerns and priorities may be quite different.

While a great deal of attention is paid to ensuring that people die "with dignity", this is usually taken to mean without pain. The instinct and training of those in hospitals are to increase analgesics (which the patient may be able to control by means of a hand-held pump) whose purpose is to avoid the distress of a painful death. But where opiates are being used to depress pain a frequent side effect is to increase drowsiness. There is nothing inherently sinister in this – although in Britain at least two cases have resulted in criminal proceedings;[12] indeed, there is much to commend. However, where patients drift into drugged comas from which they never emerge, questions frequently arise about "unfinished business"; and those questions have implications for funerals.[13]

---

idealisation or of legend. To what extent, therefore, they are historical in the sense of recording "the facts" we may exercise some doubt. While Ariès' later observations may be less open to question, his assertions on the medieval period are not without complications. We are entitled to question whether all death was as he describes it from the limited sources he draws upon. We may prefer to accept Thomas Hobbes's description (Leviathan, part 1, chapter 13) of life for the vast mass of people as "solitary, poor, and nasty, brutish and short" with its accompanying continual fear and danger of violent death. This is quite different from Ariès' more romantic vision.

10 These figures are drawn from the survey published as *Mortality Statistics: Review of the Registrar General on Deaths in England and Wales*, 1985, DH1 No.17, OPCS, HMSO, 1987, and support Ariès's contention about the predominant arena of modern death. It is not at all clear that people would prefer to die in hospital; in fact, the preferred place of death is home.

11 This later discussion will introduce further questions about control. If we concede that medical staff increasingly control the process of death, we may yet ask who controls the ritual of the funeral.

12 The first of these was *R. v Cox*, Winchester Crown Court, 1992. The accused was the doctor who administered drugs in order to end the life of a woman patient whose terminal illness was both long drawn out and extraordinarily painful. The body had been cremated before Dr Cox was charged, and so the indictment was attempted murder. Dr Cox was found guilty and received a suspended sentence. He was subsequently subject to disciplinary proceedings before the General Medical Council.
The second related to Dr Harold Shipman who was found guilty on a series of specimen charges of having murdered patients by the injection of opiates. The Shipman case resulted in two official enquiries. The first, into the deaths of others of his patients, suggested that he may have killed several hundreds. The second investigated general questions relating to the registration of deaths.

13 It ought also to be noted that it is precisely those dying with "unfinished business" whose pain, being mental/emotional as much as physical, is poorly responsive to ordinary doses of painkillers. This in turn may tempt doctors to prescribe greater and greater dosages with the attendant risk of increased drowsiness. In more straightforward cases, good pain relief does not inevitably bring such side effects.

Dying can be an opportunity for reconciliation. The preface to the orders of service for "Ministry to the Sick and Dying" in the prayer book of the Anglican Church of the Province of South Africa (1989: 489) puts it thus:

> Our Lord Jesus Christ proclaimed the coming of the kingdom of God not only by preaching but also by healing the sick. He brought healing in all its fullness: physical cures, the healing brought by the forgiveness of sin, restoration of broken relationships, assurance of salvation, acceptance of the sinner by God . . .
>
> In the ministry of healing . . . It is right and fitting to pray for healing of the body, of the mind, of the emotions, of the memories, for healing to offer relationships and society.

Where this process has been hampered by the dying person's extended unconsciousness, and where the words of sorrow and forgiveness remain unspoken and unheard, the funeral agenda is increased and the opportunity for thankfulness rather than for guilt is lost.

As the hospital takes the dying person out of the context of her/his family and friends, the management of death presents itself more and more as a technological problem. Death, however, will not go away; and the problem cannot be resolved, only delayed. While death is seen in these terms, two things follow:

–   as technical sophistication increases, the ethical boundaries are stretched; and

–   death is increasingly viewed in terms of mechanical control, and human life is defined by the same language.

In the remainder of this chapter we must address questions which medical ethics faces and give some account of how society responds to these in the legal system. In Chapter Four we shall consider the question of human identity.

The medical and legal interface

In 1986, Karen Grandstrand Gervais challenged the view that death is simply a question of biological definitions.[14] She sought to determine the conceptual framework underlying the adoption of brainstem death as an adequate delimitation of that state which distinguishes what we call a dead person from what we call a living person. Her analysis gained impetus from the fact that brainstem death was finding acceptance as a definition of death in the law courts of the United States of America. This development arose without a clear distinction between that condition and the persistent vegetative state. It was a distinction which Gervais herself was unwilling to draw.

Gervais referred to the earlier work in this field of Michael Green and Daniel Wikler (Green and Wikler, 1980: 105-133),[15] raising questions about the ontology of personhood. She began by asking what was meant by the statement "patient Jones is alive" (Gervais: 113). The two reasonable deductions were that "the patient is alive" and

---

[14]   Gervais, K. G. 1986. *Redefining Death* (New Haven, CT: Yale University Press).

[15]   Green, M. and Wikler, D. 1980. "Brain death and personal identity", *Philosophy and Public Affairs* vol. 9, no. 2.

"the patient is (remains) Jones". By saying that the patient is still (remains) Jones, we maintain that the patient retains that set of psychological traits which we have always distinguished as making up Jones.[16] What, however, if the patient is alive, but does not retain that psychological set, and nor does anyone else? Can we say that Jones no longer exists, and Jones is dead?

Here, for Gervais, is the nub of the matter:

> The circumstance in which the patient is alive, yet Jones is dead, is an uncomfortable one (ibid.).

Generally, she argues, when we talk of Jones we do not distinguish (as Green and Wikler do) between the psychological traits that mark Jones and Jones's body. Green and Wikler wish to define the aliveness of the body by reference to heart-lung criteria (that is, the continuance of a heartbeat and of respiration), while using the criterion of the psychological continuity for discerning the aliveness of the person:

> Jones's death . . . occurs *either* at the time the patient dies, if the patient has remained Jones; or at the time the patient ceases to be Jones, whichever comes first (Green and Wikler: 118).

Gervais objects that Green and Wikler's distinction obscures matters, and suggests that when we speak of Jones dying we speak of Jones ceasing to be (however caused):

> Human death is the ceasing to be of the person (Jones); after that event, talking about the life status of the body is inappropriate.

For Gervais, the differentiation made by Green and Wikler between the death of the patient and the death of Jones makes for dualism. Jones becomes an entity with the particular set of psychological traits, yet Green and Wikler do not clearly describe what that entity is which possesses such a psychological make-up. Gervais regards this as a fatal flaw.

What are we to make of those occurrences of patients who lose their distinctive set of psychological traits but whom we would not wish to describe as brain dead? If Jones were to contract Alzheimer's Disease, we might want to say that Jones's body no longer possesses Jones's psychological life, and that somehow the patient has ceased (to that extent) to be Jones. We might be less happy to conclude that Jones is dead. After all, some mental life (however diminished) continues to be supported by Jones's body. If a new person has emerged, when did this occur?

Gervais suggests that, if we were to decide that a new person has emerged, we might need to give the new person a different name and identity. Would such a person then be entitled to dispose of Jones's estate, and how would Jones's family be related to this new person? She concludes by rejecting a purely mentalist approach to personhood:

> . . . there is something important about a continuous link between body and consciousness, however altered that consciousness may be. We must resist the idea

---

[16]   Gervais' way of talking about the psychological traits of Jones seems forced. It would be easier and more natural if you were to speak of Jones's personal rites. I shall use Gervais' terminology in referring to our work, although I think that she appears to be making a distinction without a difference.

that such neural deterioration, by destroying all psychological continuity, is a sufficient condition for the death of the person. Bodily continuity must have a role in personal identity in some circumstances, then, though possibly not in all circumstances (Gervais: 118).

Furthermore, as instances of amnesia show, we are more than our memory of ourselves. Not least there are the memory and recognition that others have of us. Amnesia is not a certifiable cause of death!

> As long as Jones's body continues to function and his brain supports some set of psychological traits, the person Jones must still be regarded as alive (ibid.).

Gervais thus aligns herself with a more conservative approach which sees the human person as an embodied consciousness. What defines life is an experiencing consciousness. Death is the irretrievable failure of an organism (in this case the human organism) to be able consciously to receive and respond to stimuli. Gervais poses a moral framework for our understanding of personhood and for the definition of death which follows from it. Her intention is to offer guidelines for American public policy in medical ethics, and she concludes by redefining "brain death" as the permanent cessation of consciousness. Anyone in a persistent vegetative state should be declared dead.

Such a conclusion had no legal force, and doctors continued to be faced with the problem of how to determine death. In the United Kingdom, Professor David Short wrote a brief article on the persistent vegetative state (PVS) in which he described PVS in distinction from brain death.[17] He noted that the prognosis was poor:

> Of patients who remain in the PVS for three months, about a half die within twelve months; but some survive for fifteen years or more. One has been recorded as surviving for 36 years; sustained simply by basic nursing care and nutrition by nasogastric or gastrostomy tube. A few regain consciousness, but all remain severely physically and mentally disabled and dependent (Short: 39).[18]

Short noted that there was a move to see PVS as a form of brain death, but suggested three difficulties: the criteria for brainstem death are not fulfilled by PVS; there is no suffering (by which I presume Professor Short to mean that where consciousness is suspended there can be no suffering on the part of the patient – however distressing things may appear to onlookers); some patients do regain consciousness.

Professor Short was not making his observations in an academic vacuum. As he wrote, there was a tragic case which had been in the news for some time. It was that of Tony Bland (see below). Short's next comments were therefore not without interest, since they raised the central issue at trial in *Bland v Airedale NHS Trust*. He wrote of such patients:

> If they could make a rational decision, they might request to be allowed to die. But they have not the cerebral capacity either to make such a decision or to express it.

---

[17]   Short, D. S. 1992. "The Persistent Vegetative State", *Ethics and Medicine*, vol. 7, no. 3.
[18]   While the percentages may have changed, and the overall prognosis may have marginally improved, PVS remains (by definition) *persistent*.

He noted that in the American courts a case has been decided in which a young woman who had been in a persistent vegetative state for four years had been "allowed to die". In that case evidence had been brought by several witnesses that she had on a previous occasion "expressed wishes which had favoured withdrawal of treatment". The American Medical Association had not been able to arrive at an agreed view about how to deal with such cases, and Dr Short concluded that this was clearly a subject which required further careful consideration. Such consideration was given in a case decided in the English courts in 1992 and 1993. The issues which Gervais and Short had raised were vital.

Bland v Airedale NHS Trust

> Anthony Bland became 21 on the 21st September this year but for the past three and a half years he has been totally unaware of the world around him. As a keen supporter of Liverpool Football Club he was at the Hillsborough football ground on the 15th April 1989. He was then 17½. He was one of the victims of the disaster. He suffered a severe crushed chest injury which gave rise to hypoxic brain damage. His condition rapidly deteriorated and despite the intensive and heroic efforts of the doctors and nurses he has remained ever since in the state of complete unawareness. This is known to the medical profession as a "Persistent Vegetative State" (PVS). Although his brain stem is intact he suffered irreparable damage to cortex. All the higher functions of Anthony Bland's brain have been destroyed. There is no hope whatsoever of recovery or improvement of any kind. That is unanimous opinion of all the distinguished doctors who have examined Anthony Bland.[19]

So began the President of the Family Division of the High Court in delivering his judgement in the above case in November 1992. Since there was no hope of improvement, the question arose about terminating medical treatment. What was proposed was that the nasogastric tube by which Anthony was fed should be removed. The judge described what would happen:

> If this course were to be adopted then within some 10 to 14 days the lack of sustenance would bring to an end the physical functioning of the body of Anthony Bland and he would in terms "die". The process would be that of "starvation". This would be unpleasant for those who had to observe it but Anthony Bland himself would be totally unaware of what was taking place.

The doctor in charge of Anthony Bland contacted the coroner charged with dealing with cases arising from the Hillsborough disaster, and was advised that such a course of action might result in criminal proceedings. The hospital therefore decided to obtain a declaration from the courts that doctors could lawfully discontinue treatment and support designed to keep Anthony Bland alive. An *amicus curiae* was appointed by the Official Solicitor to represent Tony Bland's interests. Argument was brought to suggest that feeding Tony Bland was not medical treatment and that while medical treatment

---

[19] All citations relating to the various judgements in this case are drawn from the *All England Law Reports* [*AER*] 1993, vol. 1. The full report of this case occurs on pages 821-896. The extract in this reference is at page 824f-h.

might be withdrawn, feeding might not. It was submitted that to withdraw food was to act with the intention of bringing about the death of the patient, and that such an act would be unlawful – indeed, it would be murder. In each of three courts this argument was rejected unanimously by the judges (nine in all), although some were extremely hesitant about the implications of what they were saying.[20] In the House of Lords, there was a clear call for Parliament to consider legislation, since the criminal law was a poor sledgehammer for the ethical nut.

The judges were not particularly concerned to ask themselves about the nature of death in other than medical terms, although in the court of first instance the President of the Family Division said:

---

[20] For a criminal prosecution to be successful, it must be established that a criminal act (*actus reus*) has been committed with criminal intention (*mens rea*). Three different degrees of criminal intention may be possible in the successful prosecution for murder: intent to kill, intent to cause grievous bodily harm, intent to act in such a way that a reasonable person would know that either of the first two possibilities would follow. In *Bland v Airedale NHS Trust,* it was agreed that a *mens rea* was present, since the action of depriving Tony Bland of his food would inevitably result in his death. It was therefore vital to prove that the proposed course of action was not an *actus reus*.
When the case reached the House of Lords, Lord Brown-Wilkinson sought to distinguish between acts of commission and omission in defining the *actus reus*:

> As to the guilty act, or *actus reus*, the criminal law draws a distinction between the commission of a positive act which causes death and the omission to do an act which would have prevented death. In general an omission to prevent death is not an *actus reus* and cannot give rise to a conviction for murder. [*AER*, 1993: 880j].

I wrote to Lord Brown-Wilkinson, to establish whether his distinction in the *actus reus* could be replicated in the *mens rea*.

> If I push a child under a car there is an *actus reus*, if I see that same child run into the path of that same car yet fail to do anything to prevent the accident there is no *actus reus* . . . But this is not the case with Anthony Bland. The cause of death in the mind of Dr Howe, who will presumably complete the death certificate, is the set of fatal injuries that he received at Hillsborough. He has said as much in an interview televised after the House of Lords' decision. It was directly put to him that by failing to feed Anthony he was killing him. His reply was that this was not the case, Anthony's death was a result of his injuries. In Dr Howe's mind, the end of the death had been delayed . . . Could we not therefore argue that the purpose of stopping the artificial feeding is to *complete* the death of Anthony Bland rather than to bring it about. It has been brought about by [his] injuries. (Letter to Lord Brown-Wilkinson, dated 10 February 1993)

I sought in my letter to suggest that, just as the judges had found that there was no *actus reus*, so equally they could have resisted the suggestion that there was a *mens rea*. In his reply to me (dated 12 February 1993), Lord Brown-Wilkinson rebutted my suggestion by applying it to a hypothetical case of a patient who was sensate, but unable to survive without mechanical ventilation. If his ventilator were switched off by someone who stood to gain financially by his death, he would (on my proposal) avoid conviction for murder.

> The law tries to draw a distinction between the motive with which an act is done (which is irrelevant) and the intention with which the act is done. Although the motive of the doctor who removed the artificial life-support and the motive of the person who wishes to make a financial benefit out of the death are different, the intention is the same in both cases, viz. to bring about the death of a patient.
> *For myself, I believe a more fruitful line of approach is to redefine death for legal purposes as not being confined to brain stem death but also including those who have no sensate awareness of any kind and never will have.* [my stress]

If nothing else, I learnt from this exchange that it was better for liturgists not to tangle with Law Lords!

To his parents and family he is "dead". His spirit has left him and all that remains is the shell of his body.

Whether Sir Stephen Brown was a deliberate or instinctive dualist did not really matter to the resolution of *Bland v Airedale NHS Trust*, although as I shall suggest in Chapter Six the issue is highly significant for our theological understanding of human existence and has implications for the ritual agenda of funerals. Here it is sufficient to note that the difficult legal and ethical judgements which this case aroused depended upon an agreement that death (at least in this instance) was a matter of medical control.

Yet even in this case where the medical issues were central, all those who were appointed to adjudicate referred to the moral dilemma, and the language of control. A consideration of death may begin with medical questions and definitions, but it cannot end there.

One judge was prepared to tease the issue out in some detail, and I shall recount how he did this in the following chapter. The issues that he addressed move our consideration of death from the field of medical analysis to philosophical and anthropological considerations. In order to describe death we shall need to consider questions about human existence. The conclusions which we reach will shape our consideration of how death is to be confronted in the social and ritual contexts of the funeral.

CHAPTER 4

The End of Life

Hoffmann's dilemma

When *Bland v Airedale NHS Trust* came to the Court of Appeal, Lord Justice Hoffmann approached the ethical issue as matters not simply of legal jurisdiction but of a broader, widespread debate.[1] Giving judgement third, Hoffmann began by rehearsing the non-contentious detail of the case, and briefly indicated that he would concur with his colleagues in declaring that no criminal liability would arise from ceasing to keep Anthony Bland alive. He continued:

> But this case has caused a great deal of public concern. People are worried, perhaps not so much about this particular case, but about where it may lead. Is the court to assume the role of God and decide who should live and who should die? Is Anthony Bland to die because the quality of his life is so miserable? Does this mean that the court would approve the euthanasia of seriously handicapped people? And what about the manner of his death? Can it ever be right to cause the death of a human being by deliberately depriving him of food? *This is not an area in which any difference can be allowed to exist between what is legal and what is morally right.* The decision of the court should be able to carry conviction with the ordinary person as being based not merely on legal precedent but also upon acceptable ethical values. For this reason I shall start by trying to explain why I think it would be not only lawful but right to let Anthony Bland die. In the course of doing so I shall also try to explain why the principles upon which this judgement rests do not make it a precedent for morally unacceptable decisions in the future.[2]

Lord Justice Hoffmann conceded that it was an unusual procedure for a judge to argue from moral rather than purely legal principles, but he wanted to understand the case by examining the moral principles involved. In doing so he acknowledged the help he had gained from his conversations with Professor Ronald Dworkin and Professor Bernard Williams.[3] Hoffmann saw the case as resting upon a conflict between three ethical principles: the sanctity of life, the right of self-determination, and respect for the dignity of the individual. We may argue that it is almost always wrong to cause the death of another human being "even one who is terminally ill or so disabled that we may think that if we were in his position we would rather be dead" (*AER*, 1992: 851e).

---

[1]   Throughout my discussion of this case, I have referred to Lord Justice Hoffmann. The learned judge was subsequently appointed to the House of Lords, where he assumed the title Lord Hoffmann. However, at the time of *Bland v Airedale NHS Trust*, Hoffmann was a Lord Justice of Appeal.

[2]   *AER*, 1992: 850f-j. The emphasis is mine.

[3]   Professor of Jurisprudence and White's Professor of Moral Philosophy respectively at Oxford University at the time. Professor Dworkin was in the process of writing *Life's Dominion* (1993), and Lord Justice Hoffmann had also been able to read the manuscript of that book.

We may equally argue that whatever our own beliefs another person has the right to refuse treatment which might keep her alive.[4]

> A person of full age may refuse treatment for any reason or no reason at all, even if it appears certain that the result will be his death.
>
> I do not suggest that the position which English law has taken is the only morally correct solution. Some might think that in cases of life and death, the law should be more paternalistic even to adults. The point to be emphasised is that there is no morally correct solution which can be deduced from a single ethical principle like the sanctity of life or the right of self-determination. There must be an accommodation between principles, both of which seem rational and good, but which have come into conflict with each other (*AER*, 1992: 851e-f).

The importance of Hoffmann LJ's judgement for this part of our discussion is that, in setting the various moral principles against one another, the judge proceeds to show how the principle of respect for others influences not only what kind of medical provision we may offer to the dying but also the respect we pay to the dead. "We pay respect to their bodies and their memory because we think it an offence against the dead themselves if we do not" (*AER*, 1992: 854a). Such a respect meant that in the case before the court there was a conflict between the principle of the sanctity of life and the view expressed by those who knew him best that Bland would have chosen to die rather than live. In the specific circumstances of *Bland v Airedale NHS Trust* Hoffmann believed that Bland's right to self-determination was the stronger principle.

In concluding his judgement, Lord Justice Hoffmann said, "I would expect medical ethics to be formed by the law rather than the reverse". This reflects a not uncommon reluctance to allow doctors to set the ethical boundaries for themselves as they seek to exploit technical advances. When those advances relate to competence in prolonging life, the reluctance is frequently intense.

The learned judge asked whether the courts were to assume the role of God in deciding issues of life and death. His unease is shared by doctors who have to make precisely these decisions in the performance of their duties. It will not ease their burden, but it may make the critics less censorious, if we consider the possibility that it is precisely the struggle with such moral complexity that the Priestly account of Creation foreshadows in its description of human creation as being in the image of God (Gen 1.26-27) and which the Yahwist describes in talking of the Fall as in some sense involving the acquisition of moral awareness – "the knowledge of good and evil" (Gen 3.5, 22). If we accept such a reading of these Old Testament passages, then certain things follow. We cannot allow ourselves to blame others for our own errors of judgement.[5] Equally, we cannot allow others to evade their moral choices. Finally, we

---

[4] Hoffmann gave the example of Jehovah's Witnesses who refuse consent for life-saving blood transfusions.

[5] See, Thielicke, H. 1964. *How The World Began* (London: James Clarke). In this collection of sermons on Genesis 1-11, Thielicke argues that Adam blames Eve, while Eve blames the snake; neither of the protagonists admits responsibility. This, for Thielicke, is as important an issue (more, even) as the eating of the fruit, for the denial of guilt excludes grace and the possibility of forgiveness (152-170).

are all involved in the making of our ethical boundaries, which will never cater for every situation.

Codes of ethics are provisional suggestions for response to hypothetical situations; the realities mean that we often have to "play God". Our anxiety is based upon our recognition that hard cases make bad laws. Language about playing at God usually assumes that God is omniscient, infallible and static; and our own self-knowledge makes us aware that we cannot play that sort of God. We are bound to make mistakes, and the knowledge of our limitation conflicts with the image that we have of God. If, however, we admit the possibility that God may be open to change (and that such change may include change in the knowledge that God possesses), then "playing at God" becomes an invitation to join in the act of creation. Furthermore, if we understand "playing at God" in other than pejorative or hubristic terms, we may begin to understand our play as an important educational tool in which we learn from the world of imagination (or image-ing) how to live in the "real" world.[6]

If we take seriously our responsibility to make moral decisions, then the static understanding of God has to be modified to permit a more dynamic view in which God is still at work.[7] It may be easier to move from an antithetical stance in which limitation is always viewed as failure (or worse, as guilt) to more creative possibilities in which we dare to take a share in the responsibility for creating a moral universe in cooperation with and in dependence upon God.

In the context of death and bereavement, blame-finding is a catastrophic way of proceeding, since it locks us in the past with little or no hope of a new future. This progress from the past to the future is important in coming to terms with death and bereavement and in Chapters Four and Six we shall discover how ritual categories delineated in social anthropology demonstrate this and what the pastoral and theological implications are for funerals.

At the beginning of Chapter Three, I suggested that theologians had not addressed the question "What is death?"; at its close I noted that Lord Brown-Wilkinson wanted a legal definition which moved from using only brainstem death as a criterion to one which included "those who have no sensate awareness of any kind and never will have".

---

[6]   In a series of questions and answers, published in *The Independent* newspaper (London: 17 October 2002), Lord Winston, Professor of Fertility Studies at Imperial College, London, was asked, "Do you ever worry that you are playing God?" He replied:

  I've always been worried by that epithet [*sic*] because it seems to me that playing God is what we should be doing. Playing God essentially means protecting life. In that way, I don't see what the difference is between helping someone to get pregnant and saving someone's life by giving them an antibiotic. It seems to me that both those actions are equally "playing God", but that's a good thing because they promote life. *Not supplanting God is the issue* [stress mine].

[7]   Cf. Jn 5.17, where the poolside healing of the paralytic who picks up his mat and carries it away provokes a debate with the Pharisees about work on the Sabbath. Jesus refers to the continuing work of God which is to be complemented by his own work: *ho Patēr mou heōs arti ergazetai, kāgō ergazomai*.
  The scandalous implication is that the sabbath rest of God (which, the rabbis taught, God was still enjoying after his labour of creation) is not a refraining from work at all. Unlike the deities of Mount Olympus, Yahweh does not dwell in *ataraxia*; the work of bringing order out of chaos continues.
  I argue here that this continuing work includes the realm of ethics, in which human beings co-operate with (or rebel against) God in discerning good and evil.

It should not pass without comment that Brown-Wilkinson's proposal still left the crucial question in the hands of the doctors. Who is to determine whether sensate awareness is something that a given patient "never will have", if not the doctor – or those acting upon the doctor's advice?

Lord Justice Hoffmann's dilemma rests upon the difficulty of balancing competing principles relating to human life and its termination. The case of Tony Bland raises questions about how we relate personhood and the biological aliveness of a human being. For doctors and the courts a person is considered in relation to her/his physiological status; but is this an adequate way to describe human existence? When Professor Fred Feldman tackled questions of personhood and death, he approached the issues from quite different perspective.[8]

I think not, therefore I am not?

Feldman's philosophical method in describing the nature of death is to advance successive definitions which he analyses in order to discern how further refinement may be made at the next stage of the discussion. Thus, although he has no formal debating partner, Feldman's style is basically Socratic.[9] In his introductory remarks he observes that talk about death necessarily involves talk about life. Yet he resists the notion that death is simply ceasing to exist:

> When Hamlet says, "To be or not to be, and that is the question," he really means "To die or not to die, that is this the question." Hamlet apparently supposes that when a living thing dies, it stops existing – it ceases to be. Very many philosophers agree. But this "termination thesis" blatantly conflicts with some obvious facts. There actually exist very many dead bodies. Each of these formerly was alive. Hence, these seem to be things that died but did not cease to exist . . . I try to unravel this conceptual tangle (Feldman. 6).

Feldman's thesis reveals the awkwardness of biological and psychological theories of death, and his analysis demonstrates the inadequacy of biological categories to arrive at a satisfactory philosophical definition of death. The implication for Christian theology is that metaphysical inquiry is essential to its understanding of death.

When we rejoin him, Feldman has arrived at the point where he denies the truth of the statement:

> Necessarily, no biological person's history as a biological person extends beyond his or her death (Feldman: 119).

Feldman argues that the biological history of a human being transcends biological life, since the corpse has existence and is identifiably human. Moreover, he asserts, the history of their biological existence is necessarily distinct from that existence itself. However, a person's psychological existence and history may well be coterminous, and Feldman posits:

---

[8]   Feldman, F. 1992. *Confrontations with the Reaper: A Philosophical Study of the Nature and Value of Death* (New York: Oxford University Press).

[9]   His conclusions about life and death are far from Socratic.

Necessarily, no psychological person's history as a psychological person extends beyond his or her death (Feldman: 121).

Whereas, according to Feldman, corpses continue to be biological persons, though not psychological persons (Feldman: 123). The notion of biological personhood continuing beyond death is a strange one – even though the bereaved often wish to address the dead person directly. Clearly, a person's legal personality survives death in the disposition of his or her estate (whether testate or intestate). However, Feldman's category of biological existence beyond death does not seem to be saying anything other than that after death there is a corpse. He admits that "when a living thing dies, it ceases to exist as the living thing" (Feldman: 105), and this seems to me to be crucial. To speak of a corpse as having biological existence is to stretch the concept of biological existence too far. A corpse no longer has any centrally organised and sustained being; it is in decay. The examples Feldman gives of things which cease to exist yet do not die (boys who cease to be boys when they become men, caterpillars which cease to be caterpillars when they pupate, and so on) are so different in their order of existence from the gulf between life and death that they effectively invalidate his argument.

At first glance it appears that, in 1 Corinthians 15, St Paul uses a similar argument about things ceasing to exist in their old form but finding new life in different orders of existence. However, St Paul is arguing from metamorphosis in nature to the experience of the resurrection of the body which is found in Christ. This is quite a different account of how human personality survives death, and the analogies used by the apostle and by Feldman are equally distinct in their philosophical purpose. Similarly, the saying of Jesus that "unless a grain of wheat falls into the earth and dies, it remains just a single grain; but if it dies, it bears much fruit" (Jn 12.24) uses the language of metamorphosis in a metaphorical sense but to a different end. The reference in the Johannine text is not to the resurrection of the body, but to the salvation wrought by Jesus' death, and it is important to distinguish these scriptural examples of the language of metamorphosis as they relate to death from the usage of Professor Feldman.

As part of his inquiry, Feldman asks whether it is possible to define death as a punctiliar event. He draws a distinction between the process of dying (which we may describe as, for example, a slow death) and the instant when an organism passes from being alive to being dead (Feldman: 109). However, after protracted analysis Feldman is left to acknowledge:

> that death is a conceptual mystery – that it is impossible to formulate a fully satisfactory philosophical analysis of the concept of death (Feldman: 125).

> But death is profoundly destructive. Brain cells are inevitably ruined by death. Thus, death . . . does seem to mark the end of the history of an entity as a psychological person. Although a given psychological person may continue to exist for a time after death, he or she almost certainly will cease to be a psychological person when he or she dies.[10] A rotting corpse no longer has self-conscious intelligence (Feldman: 124).

---

[10]   I take this to refer to the distinction between death as a process (dying) and death as the moment of transition from life to non-life.

Feldman's concern is not with questions about whether death is a transition to some other form of life. He simply asks what death is; and his inquiry leads him to the conclusion that the biological and psychological sciences do not provide an adequate answer for philosophy.[11] In my view, Feldman's conclusion is inevitable, given that his language about personhood is unequivocally materialist. His philosophical discussion is limited by that constraint, and thus denies to him an effective metaphysical arena of discourse.

Gilbert Mury, a French Marxist, also needed an explanation of death which was wider than the biological and psychological. For him, the answer lay in a metaphysic of history:

> We do not treat the dead body as a living person, but, confronted with the body, we bear witness that not the whole of man has been destroyed.
>
> The end to personal consciousness is something intolerable. But we do not say this as an existentialist would: for us, consciousness means action. It becomes real in what it does. That is why all is not abolished. The table survives the carpenter and the "job" survives the labourer.
>
> And if all this sounds rather banal, the reason is that death itself is a banal tragedy. And even to say this is in itself banal.[12]

Mury's view is classically Marxist, and his distinction of the Marxist from the existentialist position is underlined by Heidegger's view of death as that which gives meaning, urgency and authenticity to all living.[13] Heidegger does not speak for all existentialists any more than Mury represents himself on this issue as speaking for all Marxists. Nonetheless, Mury appears to represent something of a unified Marxist tradition when he speaks of the job surviving the labourer. He understands action in the arena of history as that which validates the individual human life. The individual derives value only from her/his contribution to the socio-historical process. While death is "banal", its presence does not rob human existence and endeavour of its meaning, since these are granted or withheld by history. Heidegger, on the other hand, proposes that our lives gain their authenticity only as we experience the "nothing" of death. It is the willingness to understand our finitude and our guilt that enables us to see death as the great possibility in which we are set free. When we have seen death in this way we are released to find coherence and focus in living.

Such a view is in sharp contrast to that proposed by Feldman who discusses the value of death in purely utilitarian terms.[14] Feldman argues that death is not always bad, but suggests that there are occasions when we should see death as a bad thing. He instances the case where it deprives the individual of a good or happy life. The particular example he gives is of a boy who while undergoing minor surgery dies as a

---

[11] In the second part of his book Feldman goes on to ask questions about the value of death, and to these I shall return shortly.

[12] Mury, G. 1968. "A Marxist View of Burial. *Concilium*, vol. 2, no. 4 (February): 79-80.

[13] We ought not to classify Heidegger as an "Existentialist" without qualification. He himself would have rejected such a description.

[14] Feldman's particular attention to the issues of abortion, suicide and euthanasia, while important in other contexts, is not germane to our particular concerns.

result of an anaesthetic mishap. Since the boy might have lived happily for many more years, his death results in an extrinsic loss for him. Such a loss is bad (Feldman: 139). Feldman agrees that the death of one person may mean sadness and loss for others, but he focuses his attention upon the value death has for the dying person.

A similarly individualistic emphasis pervades Dworkin's book *Life's Dominion*.[15] Professor Dworkin seeks to chart a way for medical ethics in the contentious areas of abortion and euthanasia. Part of his task is to discover what we mean when we say that life is sacred (Dworkin: 71-81).

Heidegger's concern was to see death as the explanation of life, which enabled life to be lived more authentically. Feldman's analysis ignores death as an "explanation" of life, and describes death's value in terms of individualist utilitarianism. Dworkin describes the sacred as "inviolable", adding that it gains its inviolability from intrinsic rather than incremental value. Something is incrementally valuable if there is a direct relationship between the frequency or amount of its occurrence and the value we place upon it (for example, precious stones or metals). Intrinsic value arises from the very fact of the existence of whatever (or whoever) it is that we value.

> The hallmark of the sacred as distinct from the incrementally valuable is that the sacred is intrinsically valuable because – and therefore only once – it exists. It is inviolable because of what it represents or embodies. It is not important that there be more people. But once the human life is begun, it is important that it flourish and not be wasted (Dworkin: 73-74).

Dworkin's concept of the inviolable is based upon a value system rooted in loss; that is, what would appal us by its destruction or our deprivation of it. Given that his book is about abortion and euthanasia, this category is a considerable advantage to the general argument he wishes to make. However, it is not so clear that his category of inviolability is adequate in a discussion about human existence. He begins by talking about why great works of art are inviolable – even if they are not to any given individual's taste – and concludes that their sacredness derives from the human act of creation which produced them. When he proceeds by analogy to consider human life, his category of the sacred does not seem to amount to much more than a great degree of mutual human respect. There is no taboo in Dworkin's theory, and I am persuaded that this is because he has no adequate totem. Despite his attempt to advance arguments about life and death beyond ideas of expedience, he leaves the issue as one in which polite differences of opinion are the only guide for ethical decision-making. This is an inadequate position, since ethical judgement requires some sort of social consensus – an agreed basis of value. However sophisticated the argument, the alternative will always teeter on the age of utilitarianism; for those who espouse religious faith this is an unsatisfactory basis for proceeding.

For the Christian theologian Heidegger's approach offers more scope since his evaluation of death is not confined to advantage or expedience, but addresses questions of meaning. Helmut Thielicke concluded that:

---

[15]   Dworkin, R. 1993. *Life's Dominion: An Argument about Abortion and Euthanasia* (London: Harper Collins)

you cannot define man on the basis of his biological origin; you must define him in the light of his destiny, his goal (Thielicke: 84).

This may appear to overstate the case, but Thielicke does not suggest that humans have their biological origins other than in the evolutionary order. His concern is to deny to origin a status as the sole explanation of what it means to be human. For a reliable understanding of human existence we need to take account of both goal and origin. This is a helpful suggestion and is compatible with Heidegger's understanding that it is our end that gives meaning to our existence. It also encourages me to develop an understanding of our personhood which starts from a consideration of death. The argument will prepare the way for a reappraisal of death and resurrection in Chapter Six.

The future of the soul: *bios* and *zoe*

Within the Christian tradition the overwhelming consensus about the nature of death is that it is the separation of the soul from the body. In more recent times there has been a revolt in some theological circles against the description of human personality which talks in terms of a body and a soul. Those who have led the charge have taken their stand on Old Testament categories of thought. In particular, they have been attracted by the description of the human being as a *nephesh*.[16] It is not, they argue, that Adam *had* a soul – he *was* a soul.[17] Certainly, many of the Old Testament writers seem to have viewed the human being as a psychosomatic unity (though, of course, to use the word "psychosomatic" is to use categories of thought alien to what I am describing). Death was dreaded because it represented the end of communion with God. Sheol was a place where the dead faded away – the "soul" with the "body", and where the praise of God was no longer possible. The hope of the everlasting knowledge and worship of Yahweh lay in the continuance of the nation. This is why all the pogroms and holocausts were so serious. It was not simply the dreadful matter of the deaths of all those individuals, but the threat that, if the nation were eradicated, the covenant would become extinct and with it the knowledge and praise of Yahweh in the earth.

---

[16] The other common Hebrew word used to describe the unity of the human is *basar*. This is frequently translated 'flesh'. It would be wrong to understand *basar* as 'flesh' in opposition to 'spirit', or indeed as in opposition to *nephesh*. Indeed, *basar* can mean the visible organisation of life. Nonetheless, in the later Hellenistic period, it attracted the Greek dualistic distinction from the immortal soul. Since what I'm attempting to describe is more than the visible organisation of life, *basar* is not sufficient for my purposes. I have used *nephesh* in order to include the social dimension of the person and all her/his mental and emotional activity. The choice is not easy, and others may prefer *basar* to *nephesh*. Nonetheless for my purposes *nephesh* seems a closer conceptual fit. I discuss the matter further in Chapter Six.

[17] Raymond Brown commenting specifically on Mk 14.33b-34, makes the point in this way:

The "soul" is the whole person, the "I", as can be seen from the parallelism in a psalm verse (42.6; see also 42.12), the first line of which the Marcan Jesus is echoing:

Why are you very sorrowful [*perilypos*], my soul,
and why do you disturb [*syntarassein*] me?

Brown, R. E. 1994. *The Death of the Messiah* (New York: Doubleday, I.154)

Yet the *nephesh* solution is only partial and for two reasons. First, *nephesh* was applied to all living creatures and not simply to humans. Second, the *nephesh* tradition did not survive unchallenged. There was a development within Jewish belief as it encountered other religious philosophies (the Egyptian as well as the Greek) which introduced the notion of an alternative anthropology which talked more easily of body and soul.[18] Certainly, this would make some of the language of Daniel (for example, 12.2), of the books of Wisdom and Sirach, and of Maccabees more intelligible in its divergence from the *nephesh* anthropology.

The *nephesh* tradition confronts us with other problems: those of human particularity and distinctiveness from other creatures, and the possible danger of understanding human existence only in biological terms. However, the problems raised by the body-soul hypothesis (the devaluation of the physical world and the hierarchy of values attached to personality in which intellect always heads the race) militate against a proper acceptance either of the doctrine of creation or that of the incarnation.[19] These primary doctrines require us to see matter as of intrinsic value. The material creation is a delight to God, and the saving of the world (in Christian theology) can only be achieved by the action of God in and through the incarnate Jesus. Given these convictions, I prefer an anthropological model which sees human existence as unitary. However, I still want to make a distinction between such an understanding and a biologically reductionist view.

At the beginning of Chapter Three, I suggested that Christian tradition places a strong emphasis on death as punishment for sin. Genesis 3, in speaking of the Fall, shows how death enters the scene. When Adam and Eve are banished from the Garden, they are denied access to the tree of life. The mythic language teaches us that death is the natural result of disrupted communion with God.[20]

At the end of Romans 6, we encounter St Paul's famous aphorism that the wages of sin is death. I am not convinced that we can press this into service as quickly as others would have us believe. Saint Paul is contrasting two conditions: slavery to sin and slavery to righteousness, life outside Christ and life in Christ. His concern is to talk about holy living, and is to show that baptism into the death of Christ leads us to emancipation from sin. His conclusion is to contrast death with the life of the age to come, not with some sort of earthly life that does not end in death.

The connection between sin and death is clearer when we understand sin as alienation from God who is the source of life. In alienating ourselves from God, we separate ourselves from the source of life. In this sense the wages of sin is death; and the sting of death is precisely in this separation from God who alone in Christ has

---

[18]   Perhaps of all the Old Testament traditions it is in Wisdom that the language of the soul as a separate entity occurs most clearly. (Note that we cannot properly speak of "Judaism" before 1000 AD.)

[19]   In a 1995 film, *Angels over the Net*, in which the Dutch pastoral theologian Henri Nouwen discussed his fascination with the circus act of the flying trapeze, he made the following comment: "The body tells a spiritual story. The body is not just body, it's an expression of the spirit of the human person and the real spiritual life is an enfleshed life. That's why I believe in the incarnation. There is no divine life outside the body because God decided to dress himself in a body, to become body."

[20]   If hell is separation from God and life is dependent upon God, we need to reflect upon what sort of existence is possible in hell.

conquered sin and death. We fear death because we have separated ourselves from the source of life.

It is not clear, however, that we can say that without sin human beings would not have died. There are too many assumptions here. Is the Genesis story offering a scientific explanation of death? Or is it is trying to express the complexity of the human condition, in which we need to account for a perfect God and an imperfect world? If we adopt a less static understanding of the interaction of God with the world, we may take a less punitive view of death and see its occurrence as a reminder of our creaturely finitude. We are not eternal or immortal; that belongs to God alone. Life is sustained by dependence upon God. Where this is characterised by a communion which is openly and gladly expressed, our death becomes another occasion in which God the creator and sustainer of life shapes the world by breathing into the dust and ordering the chaos.[21]

The conceptual framework which sees body and soul not simply as separate but (by and large) in opposition comes to us in its familiar form from the philosophy of Plato-Socrates.[22] The Greek tradition which viewed the soul as immortal and the body as corrupt was for many in the post-Apostolic and Patristic periods a convenient and hospitable means of expressing a Christian anthropology. Its constant difficulty was to avoid the perils of dualism – whether Gnostic or Manichee. While acknowledging the shift in emphasis, we do not necessarily need to see the body-soul description as inferior to a "purer" *nephesh* anthropology. It is probably better to view the change as an appropriate response to a shifting anthropological understanding in the world of ideas in the centuries surrounding the birth of Christ. Our contemporary dilemma is to decide whether the body-soul model is now an essential part of Christian theology, or whether we can make a fresh appraisal of human existence in the light of contemporary scientific and philosophical categories.[23] In what follows I hope to attempt a less divided anthropology than the model most widely understood and accepted in traditional theologies.

It is in the clues given to us by Heidegger and Thielicke that I find a way to advance. Certainly, I want to construct a theological anthropology which takes full account of biological and medical science, but I am also concerned to understand human existence in terms of our destiny. Since I am further committed to understanding personhood in unitary terms, I want to speak of our life in terms of our origins as *bios* (or "biotic" life) and our life in terms of our destiny or calling as *zoe* (or "zoetic" life).

Biotic life ends with death; nothing survives. At death we lose our ambitions, our status, and our hopes, our dreams, our achievements, our wealth, our memories, our relationships, even our selves. This is to affirm that *nephesh* language is exact in its description of the end of *bios*.

---

21 Although my language about God is not one that Heidegger would have used, I think that this understanding of death is one that he would recognise as giving authenticity to life.

22 I have hyphenated these two great thinkers and made of them one, since it is frequently almost impossible to discern whether it is Socrates or Plato who speaks. Their explanation of the world is still the framework within which much popular understanding operates, whether in agreement or dissent.

23 Cf. S. Tugwell's comprehensive discussion in *Human Immortality and the Redemption of Death* (1990).

Zoetic life also ends with death. We are not immortal. Yet this end is not extinction but teleological; we move to the goal, for zoetic life is life in communion with God. At our death, we are called into a new order of being:

> The hour is coming, and is now here, when the dead will hear the voice of the Son of God, and those who hear will live. (Jn 5.25).

I intend to argue this at greater length in Chapter Six. For the present I wish only to suggest that a Christian theology is possible which avoids the body-soul anthropology.[24] I propose this because the dualist tradition reflected a theological response to the understandings of human personhood of its day, and Christian theology ought now to offer some reflection upon the understandings of our own era.

Contemporary understandings and theologies of death present the funeral liturgist with challenges in the selection of scriptures and the construction of prayers. The task of creating a rite which does not avoid the biotic but which expresses the zoetic remains largely unaddressed.

---

[24] Raymond E Brown (1994: I.198) wrote of this body-soul anthropology: "With the discovery of the Dead Sea Scrolls, the . . . view, that the background for the spirit/flesh contrast was Semitic, has now become almost axiomatic. For the OT and most of the intertestamental Judaism, spirit and flesh are not parts of the human being like soul and body, but the whole human being considered under two different aspects."

CHAPTER 5

Death in the Community

The social nature of death

> If I should go before the rest of you
> Break not a flower nor inscribe a stone,
> Nor when I'm gone speak in a Sunday voice
> But be the usual selves that I have known.
>
>> Weep if you must,
>> Parting is hell,
>> But life goes on,
>> So sing as well.[1]

Joyce Grenfell's lines remind us that death is parting, and that there is in death loss not only for the dying person but also for the bereaved. Although dying my death is something that no one else can do for me, my dying is not without wider implications.

This social dimension is what Gorer referred to in his study *Death, Dying and Mourning*. One of his conclusions was that death was not talked about, and many have repeated this assessment in the years that have followed. However, so many have said this in their discussion of death that one begins to wonder how true the comment remains. Towards the end of the twentieth century, Philip Mellor observed in his essay "Death in high modernity: the contemporary presence and absence of death":

> There is now a vast body of literature on death which has been developing over the past decade, and this trend looks set to continue.[2]

Mellor added that this did not suggest a reticence on the subject of death. The academic interest in the death studies has clearly increased greatly, but beyond that death largely remains hidden.[3] Indeed, this hidden-ness was a principal theme of Mellor's essay. He argued that part of the phenomenon of high modernity had been the sequestration of death by privatising and subjectivising our experience of it; talking about death might as much conceal as reveal it. Mellor suggested that this privatisation had meant that, as death became the province of specialists and especially of the medical professionals, so

---

[1] J. Grenfell. 1981. *Joyce: by Herself and Her Friends* (London: Macmillan/Futura).

[2] This essay opens the collection of essays edited by David Clark, *The Sociology of Death* (1993). The extract cited is found at page 11.

[3] An important exception to this hiding of death is when there are public interests or state concerns. One example of this is the death of a Head of State or other leading national figure, which usually provokes wide discussion and comment; another would be a tragedy in which many are killed. In Britain, the deaths and funerals of Diana, Princess of Wales and of the Queen Mother were instances of nationally significant people; in the United States, the destruction of the World Trade Center's twin towers was an instance of a major disaster with great traumatic consequences.

funerals no longer belonged in the public domain.[4] They in turn became private events arranged by funeral specialists. He continued:

> Because meaning has been so privatised, any attempts to construct meaning around death are inherently fragile (op. cit., 21).

This privatisation of meaning has influenced clinical studies of bereavement grief. There has been a tendency to assume that it is a psychological disorder rather than a social phenomenon. Psychiatrists have attempted to establish a pathology of grief, whereas social anthropology has described the ritual process. Grief may, of course, be both psychological disorder and social phenomenon. The two categories are not mutually exclusive.

The ways in which people react to bereavement are enormously complex, yet the work of clinicians and social anthropologists has suggested a number of common features. This chapter will introduce some of their conclusions and will attempt to explain how various individual and social responses to death and bereavement shape demands upon the rites of passage associated with death. It will also offer some suggestions as to how liturgists may try to meet these demands.

Bereavement is loss occasioned by the separation of death. We might expect this particular experience to be one principally of pain without variation. Yet not all loss is painful; and we cannot describe all bereavement as unremittingly painful without danger of oversimplification – even of falsification. Indeed, one quite normal and frequent response to the death of another is relief. This is often the case where death has been drawn out and painful. In such circumstances the bereaved often describe the death as "a blessing".

In his commentary on caring for the bereaved, J. W. Worden observed at the outset that loss implies attachment, and adds that some have suggested that the goal of attachment behaviour is the securing of a bond of affection (Worden: 7-8). Whether that particular analysis is correct or not, Worden pressed home his conviction that grief as the human response to loss was extremely widespread:

> There is evidence that all humans grieve a loss to one degree or another. Anthropologists who have studied other societies, their cultures, and their reactions to the loss of loved ones report that whatever the society studied in whatever part of the world, there is an almost universal attempt to regain the lost loved object, and/or there is the belief in an afterlife where one can rejoin the loved one (Worden: 9).

He observed that among the factors that contributed to the way in which bereavement was experienced a major consideration was how the bereaved viewed death. For example, if death was seen as final and without any hope of survival, then the loss would be differently managed from what would be the case where death was understood to be transitional.

Although individual mourners experience bereavement and the management of grief differently, they are not simply private occurrences endured *in vacuo*. The bereaved

---

[4]   Mellor's language of privatisation is not meant to describe simply an individual internalisation. The contrast is with social, public and institutional experience and expression.

knows and experiences her/his grief by reference to a set of codes and *mores* gathered from the social group to which (s)he belongs, as well as by the particular personal circumstances of the death.

Even from this brief introduction, it will be evident that pastoral and liturgical concerns will have to reflect (and attempt to address) a wide variety of expectations. There will be greater or lesser appropriateness and success as the officiant is able to identify with or enter into the universe of thought which the bereaved inhabit.[5] This task is made no easier where within the one funeral the mourners reflect different attitudes and beliefs from one another and/or from the deceased. Whatever the task of the funeral, we may have to concede that there will be ambiguities of meaning and significance among those present.

In a keynote address to the Eighteenth Congress of Societas Liturgica, held at the University of Santa Clara in August 2001, Catherine Bell considered the place of marriage and funeral rites in contemporary social and religious experience.[6] She observed that, broadly speaking, religions fell into one of two categories: world-maintenance or world-renouncing (Bell: 20). Another way of describing this difference would be to talk of tribal religions in contrast to salvation religions.

> While tribal religion is the culture, salvation religions may be at war or at least in tension with the culture. Once a salvation religion becomes socially widespread and culturally dominant, it must contend with tribal practices in a new way (ibid.).

Bell observes that this leads to a tension or paradox. Noting that weddings and funerals are occasions where the family (the clan) gathers, she observes:

> It is these simultaneously intimate and clan rituals that will bring even the most decidedly secular and unaffiliated Christians back to church to use its services. Despite the plethora of models in the media and larger society of totally secular ways to marry and to bury, these are the occasions when most Americans still turn to the ritual resources of whatever religious tradition with which they feel acquainted. But once back in church, they want to put their own personal impress on tradition. They want the institutional structures that formally recognise the social transition *and* they want a personal, often idiosyncratic expression of the import of the rite to them and their loved ones (Bell: 23)

Funeral officiants know this only too well. Frequently the tension is extremely high between the liturgical forms, which talk about salvation, and the expectations of the mourners that the deceased should be honoured above all things – even above the worship of God. Many mourners want the funeral to celebrate the life of the deceased; any suggestion that it might be part of the agenda to talk about judgement – or even just about God – will be seen as a slight interruption of things. "Try not to go on too long" is

---

[5] How we may derive criteria of "appropriateness" and "success" demands a more detailed discussion than can be offered here. However, I have in view a consideration of the task of a funeral, and how such a rite (or rites) may facilitate or impede that passage from the old world of the living in which the dead person was once a member to the new world of the living in which the dead person is no longer a member. Part of this discussion will concern the social anthropology of rites of passage; the remainder will be dealt with when I introduce the detailed consideration of selected liturgies.

[6] Bell E. 2002. "Ritual Tensions: Tribal and Catholic", *Studia Liturgica*, vol. 32, no. 1: 15-28.

the request, "we're not very religious." Despair may be an understandable clerical response, but Bell's paper suggests that funerals are really part of tribal religion and at best we can "exert a rather light touch on rites so intrinsic to the tribal sphere" (Bell: 27).

Professor Bell gave her address to a liturgical congress, but noted that she was herself a ritualist rather than a liturgist. Her observation of the tensions and paradoxes arose out of the American scene, and to this extent she may reflect a higher level of continuing use of religious marriage and funerary rites than is to be found in Western Europe. In Britain church weddings are on the decline as other providers offer more photogenic or exhilarating settings.[7] However, clergy lead a very high percentage of funerals.[8]

Bell's comments about the felt tensions are well made; her conclusion that a salvation religion can only exercise a light touch on the tribal nature of funerals may be more controversial. Some will agree with Bell; they will believe that she is doing no more than describe the realties of the situation. Others will ask whether we should be content with "the realities"; they will want to resist and will argue that in ministering to the situation they cannot in conscience ignore the reality of God as part of that situation.

If tribal religion wants to re-establish the status quo and seeks to get "back to normal", salvation religion offers a critique of that world-maintenance view by suggesting, if not a renunciation of the world, at least a transformation of it.

The psychology of bereavement: a critique of "back to normal"

Colin Murray Parkes is often regarded as one of the pioneers in the field of the clinical psychology of bereavement. His book *Bereavement* (first published in 1972) has become a major text in this discipline, and subsequent researchers have felt bound to refer to his work.[9] Parkes identified three stages in bereavement grief; he described these as numbness, pining, and disorganised despair (Parkes: 27).[10]

The value of such categories lies in the taxonomy of grief by which the clinician or counsellor is enabled to recognise the various forms and moods which grief takes. Yet it would be inappropriate to understand them as separate, self-contained, sequential mood-states. Frequently those who are bereaved move back and forth between these conditions. There are times of numbness which invade pining and despair and vice

---

[7]   Bungee-jumping, sub-aqua diving, sky-diving, all feature as options for couples seeking adventurous nuptial scenarios.

[8]   In part this may be to do with the Church of England's position as an Established Church – even though more now occur at funeral chapels rather than in the local church.

[9]   Parkes, C. M. 1986. *Bereavement: Studies of Grief in Adult Life* (London: Penguin, 2nd edition). The studies which Parkes undertook in London and in Boston, Massachusetts, were among widows. This is a very specific sub-group of the bereaved; and as van Gennep remarked in *The Rites of Passage*: "it does seem right that widowers and widows should belong to this special world [between the living and the dead] for the longest time".

[10]   Elizabeth Kübler-Ross was the American pioneer in this field, and she produced similar taxonomies of bereavement grief. What is important to note here is not that there are minutiae of difference between Parkes and Kübler-Ross, but the fact of schematisation. I have referred to Parkes's work here, but in another context I might just as easily have used the work of Kübler-Ross.

versa. Fluctuations in mood can be both rapid and violent. Even after a considerable lapse of time (at least a year, sometimes many years), those who are left may occasionally experience unbelief ("Sometimes I still can't believe he's dead"), or attacks of intense pain triggered by events that often appear to be otherwise insignificant.[11]

Numbness should not be confused with the Novocain tingling of the dentist's anaesthetic; it is quite simply no feeling at all. As Parkes describes numbness, it includes that sense of disbelief which cannot take in what has occurred. Before the death this disbelief frequently manifests itself in concealment of the impending disaster from the dying person.[12] After the death there is frequently an almost frenzied busy-ness, which is compounded by the administrative tasks surrounding the official notification of death. Often this welter of activity enables the mourner to avoid dwelling on the reality of what has occurred (Parkes: 84-86).

The avoidance of thinking about what has happened – "distancing" – is a frequent strategy for coping with early sharpness of grief, and it certainly can ease the initial anguish. Where this distancing is prolonged into persistent denial and flight, the ensuing management of grief is less likely to encourage a healthy emergence from the trauma of bereavement.[13]

Pining may involve a search for the lost/dead person. Alarmed arousal and tension are typical mood-states. Mourners may become so preoccupied with thinking of the one they have lost, that they create a vivid, imaginary world in which the dead person acquires a continuing existence with developing habits and characteristics as though they were indeed still alive. At the same time the bereaved may lose interest in personal appearance and other matters which normally occupy attention. Instead, they concentrate on places and associations where the lost person might otherwise (i.e., if not dead) be likely to be found – even calling for the lost person by name (Parkes: 67).

Of course, few or none of these things may happen. It is well to remember that the psychological norms which Parkes and others describe are in effect statistically derived averages. Individual mourners may be acting well within their own normalities without necessarily falling within the apparently clear clinical boundaries. We need to question any assumption that people are made in the likeness of the statistic rather than in the image of God, who transcends all numerical analysis.

Clinical observation has led psychologists to identify a range of reactions within grief which cover the emotional, physical, cognitive, and behavioural patterns of

---

[11] An example of an "insignificant" trigger-event was experienced by my wife (albeit not at so great a distance from the event), when she was with friends at a restaurant. A drink she had ordered came to the table with a "bendy" plastic straw; she burst into tears, and just pointed. Fortunately, I realised what the trouble was. The straw was identical in style and colour to those employed in the hospice where her mother had died. These straws were used to help patients to take their morphine in solution by mouth. For my wife an enjoyable evening had, without warning, been invaded by her mother's death.

[12] This concealment is quite often a two-way process. The minister may be invited in the course of pastoral visitation not to tell "George", only to be asked by "George" not to tell the family! The concealment is always well-intentioned; it is not always conducive to a good resolution of the pain felt by all in the situation.

[13] Denial is perhaps best characterised as a refusal (conscious or otherwise) to accept the fact (in this case, of death); flight may be understood as a refusal to accept the consequences arising from that fact.

bereaved people (Worden: 22-30). When grief is analysed in such a way, we may
reasonably ask whether bereavement grief is in effect a form of depressive illness.
However, clinicians and psychologists resist too simplistic an identification. For while
there is evidence of similarities in the disturbance of sleep and of appetite as well as in
the intense sadness, there is one major difference.

> [I]n a grief reaction, there is not the loss of self-esteem commonly found in most
> clinical depressions. That is, the people who have lost someone do not regard
> themselves less because of such a loss (or if they do, it tends to be for only a brief time.
> And if the survivors of the deceased experience guilt, it is usually guilt associated
> with some specific aspect of the loss rather than a general, overall sense of culpability
> (Worden: 30).[14]

It is important, therefore, to distinguish between grief and depression as the root
causes of similar behavioural patterns. In the situations where there are no excessive
dysfunctional complications such as hallucination or obsessive treasuring of objects or
places associated with the deceased, we can still see sufficient similarities which will
prompt us to recognise the needs of those who mourn the death of those they love.[15]

The ways in which grief is expressed depend upon a range of factors beyond the fact
of the death that has occurred. Worden notes as significant the nature and depth of the
relationship between the mourner and the deceased; the nature of the death – whether
due to natural causes, an accident, suicide or homicide; how the bereaved copes
generally with anxiety and stress, and whether there is any previous experience of
bereavement; whether there are any religious or cultural affiliations with accompanying
expectations of behaviour or of support; and whether there is any other stress in the
bereaved's life apart from the bereavement. All these, he suggests, may affect the
progress and eventual outcome of grief (Worden: 32-34).

What all this demonstrates for pastoral theology and liturgy is that in the funerary
provisions we offer there has to be an intense sensitivity to the fragility of the living
whom we serve. In the vast majority of cases, those closest to the dead person are
deeply traumatised. Although the minister may address herself or himself to the needs
of the living, there need not be undue surprise at the failure of funerals to achieve a final
resolution of the grief of those who mourn. It may be that clergy do not and ought not to
expect such a resolution.[16]

---

14 One particular example of guilt among bereaved people is where they have survived an event in which
others have died. Survivors often talk of feeling guilty simply for having survived.

15 A mourner who is experiencing disturbed sleep and appetite is likely to be physically low, and the funeral
catches the bereaved when such a low may be accompanied by a deep emotional trough. Even in those
cases where the funeral is seen primarily as a rite for the bereaved, it ought to be noted that they may not
easily be able to participate; there may well be unfinished business.

16 Talking to a colleague from Zambia, I was unsurprised to discover that the grief process relating to death
was far less problematic than in the United Kingdom in particular and Western society in general.
Because death is not privatised, and because there is a strong sense of family and community, the
bereaved are supported and enabled to express their grief openly and without embarrassment. A
psychological release occasioned by that public expression contrasts with the frequently encountered
neurosis and long-term recovery prevalent among mourners who are expected to keep quiet about their

However, there may be an important task of explanation in the course of pastoral visitation before the funeral. Ministers may need to speak to mourners about how the Christian faith contemplates death and bereavement. Pastors may acknowledge the limitations of people to respond in other than partial or diminished ways in the immediate aftermath of death, and yet they may want to talk about how death challenges our values and assumptions. Rather than re-establishing the old normality (the apparent aim of some counsellors), there may be a challenge to discover resurrection in new and transformed ways of living.

Frequently the funeral is the only ritual occasion within which death and bereavement are addressed.[17] We need to be realistic about what can be achieved on a single occasion which is frequently limited to less than half an hour.

Where grief is aggravated by additional complicating factors, the pastoral agenda is itself intensified. Before Parkes's work on bereavement was published, John Hinton had recorded his own psychiatric observations of death and bereavement (*Dying* [2nd edition], 1972). He noted that the sense of loss occasioned by death was related to emotional links that existed in life. Where those ties had been very close and love had been possessive, Hinton held that the fear of death could quickly become morbid. He wrote:

> Undue emotional dependence easily gives rise to a sense of resentment too disturbing to contemplate. It is distressing to feel angry, frustrated or irritable towards the person who is so needfully loved. In this emotional climate fears for the safety of the loved person can arise; there are torturing thoughts that the needed one will die, which seems to be the worst thing that could happen (Hinton: 29).

Parkes's work confirmed Hinton's view that a strong emotional attachment in life produced deep reactions in grief. In a joint study at Harvard, he observed among widows in Boston, Massachusetts that:

> intense yearning for the dead person in the early weeks of bereavement predicted chronic grieving later (Parkes: 143).[18]

He also affirmed what Worden later described. Conflict in more than one area in a marriage complicates the grieving process (Parkes: 155). Moreover, while distancing

---

loss, to internalise it and to "get back to normal" by making themselves busy about many things. They become like Martha; often the bereaved really need to imitate Mary, who found the one thing needful.

[17] It is, of course, true that in one sense death forms part of the eucharistic liturgy insofar as it is a celebration of the paschal mystery. Further, in much evening hymnody there are references to death. However, much of this focus is distanced, so that the worshipper is unlikely to think of her or his death on these occasions other than in pietistic terms. In traditions where it occurs, praying the rosary attends to death in a more direct and particular way – both in the Sorrowful Mysteries and in the first Glorious Mystery, which may be said at the Reception of the Body into Church. Yet for most people who attend a funeral – even regular Christian worshippers – this is the primary occasion on which they confront the fact of mortality.

[18] Parkes cites a widow, who had expressed a strong sense of her husband's presence amounting almost to indwelling – "My husband's in me, right through and through. I can feel him in me doing everything" (Parkes: 107) – as grieving "intensely for several years after the death of her husband" (Parkes: 143).

the event is a way in which the journey through grief can be undertaken step by step, repressing grief is counter-productive (Parkes: 158-159).

A series of seminars and consultations with clergy and ordinands on the issue of funerals has revealed universal awareness that the expression of grief is in some way therapeutic. All have known that repression is not helpful; but this has been almost entirely an intellectual recognition. Nearly all have admitted that there have been occasions where the strong expression of emotions has caught them out and has made the situation difficult to handle. This is a rare occurrence, but it is noteworthy simply because officiating clergy learn to distance themselves by adopting a professional *persona*.[19]

There is a contemporary dread which is frequently expressed among bereaved people about "letting go". They fear that the emotion of the occasion may overwhelm them and that they may break down. To some degree this arises from expectations about keeping a "stiff upper lip" and putting "a brave face" on things.[20] To express grief by any more than wiping away a quiet tear with a handkerchief, or blowing one's nose, has been seen as letting the side down. Any further weeping is often described as "uncontrollable".

For ministers the problem is not really that these judgements spill over into pastoral attitudes; most officiants are well aware that expressing grief can be liberating. Where they find difficulty is in coping with the conflicting emotions aroused in them on such occasions.

There is the "professional" job to be done of presiding over the rite of passage on behalf of the wider social group and being the capable and efficient administrator of that rite. Equally, there is the pastoral impulse to come to the aid of the distressed in immediate compassion. It is extraordinarily hard to stop the whole funeral in order to deal with the grief of someone who does break down. There are difficulties of time – especially at crematoria – and of perceived social appropriateness, which might easily be regarded as infringed by any hiatus in the "main" proceedings.

Another potential social embarrassment is caused where some members of the family express their grief while others keep silent, or where the family remain silent but another person cries out. The embarrassment is felt because of an implicit challenge to the public hierarchy of grief which may hide a private agenda – for example, where the husband is silent but a son weeps, or where the wife is silent but the deceased's mistress cries aloud.

Such conflicts cannot be easily resolved to the satisfaction of all; clergy know this, and some become anxious when one arises. They feel threatened by the twin demands

---

[19] Since 1990 I have sought opportunities to visit theological colleges, in-service training conferences, and ministers' meetings in order to discover prevailing attitudes and beliefs.

[20] While these considerations are stereotypically white, middle-class and English, they are not exclusively confined to that conventional grouping. There is, however, a twofold shift from the stereotype: more and more people are aware of the need to express grief; and fewer and fewer people are judgemental of those who do "give way" – there is often a deep sympathy and understanding, even where it is awkwardly articulated.

of detachment and empathy, and in such circumstances feel things "going out of control".[21]

Social anthropology and death: rites of passage

If my death is something that no other individual can undertake for me, it is equally true that the death of any person is not simply a private event. Death is more than a biological phenomenon; it is a social event. When someone dies, there is a disruption in relationship. Jennifer Hockey stresses the social nature of death by reference to its accompanying ritual:

> If the "success" of death ritual can be discussed at all usefully, it is with respect to its power to express and to recreate a society's central values in a convincingly authentic fashion. Current dissatisfaction in the West with death and mourning ritual, coupled with nostalgic glances towards exotic or bygone forms, reflects the persistence of this requirement. (28-29)[22]

Hockey then offers a survey of how the historical development in our cosmological understanding has repercussions for our social codes as we try to make sense of death and the accompanying rites of passage. What follows is a summary of her argument.

The revolution introduced by Galileo, Copernicus and Kepler defined the quantifiable aspects of the world in mathematical terms; nature was reduced to shape, number and motion. This was followed by Descartes' analytical contribution which effectively overturned the mediaeval integrative world-view. The Cartesian analytical framework has predominated in the subsequent three centuries. Newton's mechanical construct of the world and Locke's theories of individualism were based on rationalism, and the mechanical view of the universe developed into a rational view of the individual. The mediaeval world-view saw God as ubiquitously immanent; the rationalist approach saw God as distinct and separate.

The mechanical-rationalist approach has led us to a medical model which is based upon Linnaean analytical taxonomy, and which is itself primarily mechanical and concerned with laws of control and motion. The mediaeval linguistic and conceptual link between "health" and "holy" has all but disappeared. However, the more recent movements of feminism, ecological concern, holistic medicine, and even

---

[21] Where the funeral is for a regular member of the congregation (or where those closest to the deceased are regular members) and where the service is in the church or chapel, some clergy feel more able to "keep control", and are able to minister to the immediate expression of grief without fear of losing others present. It ought also to be noted that expressed grief is often catching. One weeper may trigger another – possibly, the officiant, who may thereby endanger her/his professional *persona*.

In her essay "The acceptable face of human grieving? The clergy's role in managing emotional expression during funerals", Jennifer Hockey records the comments of clergy in this area. While all acknowledged the need for grief to be expressed, there were some who set limits which they would not allow the mourners to overstep. Hockey observes that clergy find disruption not simply problematic, but threatening. (Clark (ed.). *The Sociology of Death*: 129-148; particularly on this point, 130-135).

[22] Hockey, J. 1990. *Experiences of Death: An Anthropological Account* (Edinburgh: Edinburgh University Press)

fundamentalism (Christian and Islamic) are forms of rejection of the analytic-rationalist construct (Hockey, 1990: 60-62).

While this summary is an abstract of an already abbreviated over-view of the philosophical shift characterised as the Enlightenment, its broad outline can serve here as a basis for proceeding. The strong emphasis on analysis and rationalism has produced an understanding of the individual which in turn has privatised religious belief.[23] In such an atmosphere the absolute truth claims which lie at the heart of most religions may be either accommodated by relativism ("If that's what you want to believe, then that's fine for you"), or simply rejected as making no sense. The claim of the Judaeo-Christian tradition that

> To Yahweh belongs the earth and all it holds,
> the world and all who live in it (Ps 24.1)

is judged to be not simply meaningless, but presumptuous. Religious leaders are frequently enjoined to refrain from comment or action which is perceived to be beyond their competence. The underlying assumption is that there is an unbridgeable gap between the sacred and the secular. In today's terms the prophetic outbursts of Amos are not just embarrassing, they are meddlesome. Religion is about the soul, politics about the real world; and the two should be kept separate.

It is small wonder, then, that at the funeral there is a strong element of the private world of the family. The distancing, which often occurs at funerals, reinforces this. Other members of the congregation sit apart from the family;[24] and announcements in the local paper frequently reinforce this with notices requesting "Family flowers only".[25] Families often feel that "too many" flowers can be a waste of money, and prefer to invite donations to charitable causes which may be understood to mark the deceased's life and death more fittingly. There is much to commend this practice in terms of cost-effectiveness, but this is not the whole story. Whereas cards and letters can express the condolences of the wider group of mourners to the closer circle, flowers are an expression made directly to the dead person(s). Where death has occurred in a particularly tragic way, and where members of the public outside the circle of acquaintance have felt moved, the placing of floral tributes at the site has become a way in which even complete strangers may express their feelings. When funerals are made domestically "private", friends of the deceased, who are frequently closer than kith and kin, are easily excluded. The consequent emphasis upon the family reduces death to an event tied to the bloodline (and the spouse or partner). It is friendship (both within and beyond the family) which reinforces the relational nature of human existence, and which affirms the social nature of death.

Funerals are not simply private occasions without societal references; and it is the social codes surrounding death which in turn inform the rites and ceremonies of death. The shift from the mediaeval world-view has changed our expectations of what should

---

[23]   This view is supported by Mellor, "Death in high modernity", and Sennett, *The Fall of Public Man*.

[24]   People would be shocked to imagine that they were doing anything other than showing respect. The intention is to avoid intrusion and to respect privacy, but the effect may be to isolate.

[25]   Cf. J. Hockey (1990: 48).

occur at a funeral. Where death and dying are seen in terms of medical control or the loss of it, it is increasingly difficult to discern "the everlasting arms" (Deut 33.27) to which the funeral rite refers.

Hinton, writing in 1967, commented on this divergence from the Christian rite in the following succinct manner:

> If our society wholly accepted traditional Christian beliefs, there would be a general conviction that death was vanquished. In fact, in England about a quarter of the population disclaim any religious belief and about a half do not believe in an after-life (Hinton: 37).

We do well, therefore, to consider what rites of passage seek to achieve. It was van Gennep who pioneered the work in this field.[26] He identified three phases in such rites:

- rites of separation – *preliminal*;
- transition rites – *liminal*; and
- rites of incorporation – *postliminal* (van Gennep: 11).

The *limen*, or doorway, is something that must be passed through, and represents a chaotic interlude between two worlds. The control of the chaos is the task of the one who presides at the rite of passage.[27]

When he first considered funeral rites, van Gennep anticipated that it would be the element of separation which was most clearly expressed. His study of the data, however, led him to a different and surprising conclusion. Separation rites were few in number; what predominated were transition rites which were many and complex (van Gennep: 146).

Joan Littlewood summarises van Gennep's work on the three phases of rites of passage as it applies to funerals: separation removes the dead person and the bereaved from the living members of society; transition moves the dead from the world of the living towards the world of the dead, and moves the living from the world of the dead back towards the world of the living; incorporation places the dead into the world of the dead, and places the living into the world of the living.[28]

What now becomes clear is that, anthropologically speaking, the funeral is a rite of passage both for the dead and for the bereaved. This understanding is crucial for the remainder of this book. It will also be a factor in the liturgical commentary of Volume II.

In 1965, Geoffrey Gorer described the ritual of grief in contemporary Britain, and observed a number of changes in the post-war social codes relating to death. He argued

---

[26] Gennep, A. van (transl., M. B. Vizedom and G. L. Caffee). 1960. *The Rites of Passage* (London: Routledge and Kegan Paul).

[27] In the Judaeo-Christian tradition the control of the primeval chaos is the task of God, who brings out of the void order and form. I believe that this has great significance for the conduct of funeral rites. In Chapter Seven, I shall give extended consideration as to how van Gennep's analysis can be combined with the Easter *triduum* to offer a pastoral and theological framework to funeral rites.

[28] J. Littlewood. 1992. *Aspects of Grief: Bereavement in Adult Life* (24, Table 4). Littlewood offers the same analysis in her essay "The denial of death and rites of passage in contemporary societies", *The Sociology of Death* (ed. Clark: 75).

that the decline in religious belief and ritual in general had removed an important source of guidance for mourners and society at large in the social expression and management of grief. This change he regarded as both significant and unhelpful.[29]

Not all commentators agree with Gorer's conclusions as to the helpfulness or otherwise of past observances, yet it is generally acknowledged that there is no common social code referring to death in contemporary Britain. As Parkes observes, the old quarantine is gone,[30] and there is no social norm or expectation to guide either the bereaved or society at large in their meeting with one another (Parkes: 179-180).

But beyond the chances of encounter in the world of the living, the lack of an agreed social code of universal values and meanings leads to a sense of meaninglessness in the ritual of mourning. "Where there is no vision the people perish" (Prov 29.18); where there is no agreed code of meaning and value, people go to pieces.

This lack of social agreement in the realm of values as they relate to the dead has much to do with the psychological privatisation of religious belief. Faith has become compartmentalised and religious enquiry is regarded as intrusive. Religion is seen as one possible way of expressing the emotion of loss and grief, but by and large its account of what has occurred is perceived as inadequate. The general public consensus is that to know what has happened we must turn to medical and psychological models.

Yet, as we saw earlier, even here all is not well. Medical models, like their psychological counterparts, turn out to be inadequate since they belong to those explanations of the world which are analytical and which relate to mechanical control. The metaphysical question remains unanswered. Religious answers to the metaphysics fail because they do not speak in terms appropriate to the conceptual framework of most people asking the questions. Such a framework demands a demonstrable knowledge, offering control of what seems beyond control and resolution of what is apparently beyond resolution (cf. Hockey: 58). Yet death is not something we can control or resolve, and part of the theological attempt to address death is the recognition that death represents the sharpest and most intense expression of our finitude.

We have already noted that some infer from the psychologists that part of the task of funeral rites as they relate to the bereaved might be to reincorporate the mourners within the world of the living in such a way that mourning may result in a new normality which is, as it were "normality without the deceased". There are two problems here: one for social anthropology, the other for Christian theology.

---

[29] Gorer gave an autobiographical account of how in introducing himself as a mourner embarrassed others: "I wore a black tie for about three months. I had great pleasure in seeing real friends, but was unwilling to meet strangers. A couple of times I refused invitations to cocktail parties, explaining that I was mourning; the people who invited me responded to this statement with shocked embarrassment, as if I had voiced some appalling obscenity. Indeed, I got the impression that, had I stated that the invitation clashed with some esoteric debauchery I had arranged, I would have had some understanding and jocular encouragement; as it was, the people whose invitations I had refused, educated and sophisticated though they were, mumbled and hurried away. *They clearly no longer had any guidance from ritual as to the way to treat a self-confessed mourner* [emphasis mine]; and, I suspect, they were frightened lest I give way to my grief, and involve them in a distasteful upsurge of emotion" (Gorer: 14).

[30] Quarantine is derived from the Italian *quarantina* (forty), the number of days for the seclusion of widows at one time in that country.

In terms of rites of passage, we have to be very clear that the "new" normality is indeed new. A return to the old normality is physically impossible (the dead are dead), and psychologically dangerous. The psychiatric counsellor knows full well how unsatisfactory regression is. Moreover, a return to the old is a failure to pass through the ritual doorway.

The temptation of many is to dismiss ritual as being empty of meaning and value. To describe one as a ritualist is commonly held to be pejorative.[31] However, Professor Tom Driver of Union Theological Seminary argues that ritual is far from empty (Driver, *The Magic of Ritual*, 1991). Rather, ritualisation is the way by which we learn to make meaning and sense.

> Everything points to the supposition that our remote ancestors were ritualising before they became human. This activity became the pathway to the human condition. Ritualisation is a way, an experimental way, of going from the inchoate to the expressive, from the sheerly pragmatic to the communicative. Hence, in humans, it is a close relative of art, especially the performing arts. In fact, we had best think of it as their progenitor, and as the source also of speech, of religion, of culture, and of ethics. It is not as true to say that we human beings invented rituals as that rituals have invented us (Driver: 31).

If Driver is right, then ritual has the capacity to effect change where it is properly enacted. Victor Turner argued that ritual was a social drama enacting the tensions, changes and dilemmas confronting the participants,[32] and while some commentators question the performative nature of ritual there is a continuing stream of scholarship which is persuaded by the general proposition.

There are those who would argue that rituals in themselves have no substantial performative effect. Ritual is simply the execution of patterned activity that social groupings develop for various occasions. If we ask why such patterning develops, we may be satisfied to observe that a sequence occurs as one person simply copies what another has done. I tap the trunk of the sacred tree because the person immediately in front of me has done so. Such a tapping over a number of years gives the tree its sacred nature. As to why it was tapped in the first place, we cannot be certain and explanation is merely conjectural.

For the ethnographer such an approach enables us to describe ritual activity without prejudicing our account by importing our own categories of meaning. However, we may wonder whether this attempt to recover the status of detached observer is not in itself prejudicial if it fails to acknowledge that the presence of the observer is itself a new factor in the event being observed. The fly on the wall is a part of the scene.[33]

---

[31] A similar "name calling" accompanies the word "psychological". When people say that something "is just psychological", they are commonly suggesting that it has no real weight or meaning – worse, they may be suggesting that someone whose suffering they have described as "just psychological" is simply malingering.

[32] Turner, V. 1969. *The Ritual Process: Structure and Anti-Structure* (Chicago: Aldine).

[33] A similar debate arises when journalists are asked whether they provoke or simply report events. Nearly always they argue that they report and have no other function. The fly on the wall documentary on television assumes that the camera changes nothing. This seems to me to be naïve; the camera is itself an

In drawing conclusions from our observations (and there is surely little point in recording our observations for others if we do not also draw conclusions), we categorise, classify and pattern not so much to explain to the participants what they are doing as to do so for other observers and commentators. We look for meaning in what we observe.

That meaning may, indeed, be extraneous to what is ritually enacted in the sense that the actions themselves do not define what the participants believe to be happening beyond the immediate event. Indeed, as beliefs change, it may be that ritual activity lags behind.

For example, throwing earth onto the coffin is no different *as an action* for either a theist or an atheist. The reason for the action may, however, be variously explained. An atheist may use the formula "dust to dust, ashes to ashes", but the accompanying phrase – "in sure and certain hope of the resurrection to eternal life" – is clearly theist. The words offer an account of the reason for the action.

Where ritual action is accompanied by a spoken formula, it may not be unfair to regard the formula as part of the ritual action. If we make such an assumption, we may need to ask whether a traditional formula which accompanies an action eventually prompts the need for a new action for those to whom the formula is a nonsense.

In the case of throwing earth onto the coffin, can the action be entirely detached from its accompanying formula? Jayne Wynne Willson gives a great deal of practical advice for the conduct of "funerals without God" including various forms of words which may be used. "Dust to dust" is not included (though other phrases from the Hebrew scriptures are suggested).[34] While advice is given about committal at a crematorium, little is said about burial. In part this may be because at the crematorium the mechanical disposal of the coffin is remotely achieved and the advice offered is about the psychological effect on the bereaved of leaving curtains open or closed. There is, understandably, no commentary about what the committal effects other than the disposal of mortal remains. Yet the question remains: what are we doing at a burial when we throw earth onto the coffin? And does the action change its meaning according to any accompanying verbal formula? If so, is the action itself non-performative? If the action is indeed non-performative, does it require any explanatory formula? Or do we need to find meaning in what we do?

My own view is that action and meaning cannot be separated in ritual, and that we need to explain to those who come to us for funeral rites both what we do and why we do it. In this way we begin to clarify what is necessary, what is possible and appropriate and where the boundaries lie for us and for them. Of course, this assumes that there are boundaries. Some might urge that boundaries are exclusive and that we have no right to exclude the dead and the bereaved. Pastorally, we will want to be as wide in our sympathies as we can be and to be as accommodating in our help as possible. This much we freely admit. Yet this is not all there is to say. We do not come to our ministry

---

addition to the scene. If it were not there, the scene would be different. The introduction of an additional factor changes the equation.

[34] For example, an extract from Ecclesiastes 3: "To everything there is a season, and a time to every purpose on earth . . . a time to be born, and a time to die" (Willson: 26)

without our own integrity. The Christian officiant cannot say that Jesus is accursed (1 Cor 12.3). Our task is to entrust the living and the dead to the love of God in Christ. To omit this is not a course we can pursue without failing in our ministry. The Christian funeral may include a solemn farewell, but it is more than that alone.

Douglas Davies talks of the power of words and speaks of a rhetoric of bereavement.[35] He develops Maurice Bloch's categories of 'rebounding violence' and 'rebounding conquest'[36] with his own theory of 'words against death'. Davies refers to Christian baptism, which instantiates new life that does not end in death, and the eucharist, which nourishes that life; these rites have at their heart 'words against death'.

> There can be no silent baptism – words are necessary just as they are for the central act in the Mass or Eucharist where words are directly linked to the bread which is to become the 'body' of Christ. Here, once again, we encounter the performative utterance at the heart of Christian ritual (Davies, 1997:19).

Performative utterance was initially described by J. L. Austin,[37] who noted that certain phrases were in effect performances: "I name this ship", "I pronounce you man and wife" and so on. In funeral rites there are, argues Davies, similar performative utterances and these gather to themselves the proclamatory force or 'words against death'. These utterances are both formal and formative and are derived from the community of faith (Davies, 1997: 131).

Davies, Bloch and Driver all argue that the performative power of ritual and ritual words articulates a dimension of personhood beyond the biological. As persons we need ritual to express who we are – and perhaps, I would suggest, never more so than when we are confronted by death.

The implications for funeral rites are important, even if we only understand the potential for change to exist among the living. If we believe that the rite has implications for the dead, then a profoundly different agenda emerges. When we come to consider the history and theology of early Christian funeral rites, we shall see how the dead person was the focus of the liturgy. This emphasis has been forgotten in many contemporary funerary rites, and our forgetfulness has profound implications for those who mourn.

For Christian theology, going back to the old ways cannot be an appropriate response to death. The call of God is ever to new paths of life, to conversion.[38] Death is answered by resurrection, which is not an endless experience of present modes of life or even adjustments to old patterns, but a radical reordering which may find its best analogy in the language of second birth or new creation (cf. Jn 3; 1 Cor 15; Rev 21). This represents a new category, or order, of living. When Mary encounters Jesus risen from the dead, she is told, "Do not cling to me" (Jn 20.17). The new cannot be held or contained by the past; part of the liturgical agenda is to effect the separation.

---

[35] D. J. Davies. 1997. *Death, Ritual and Belief* (London: Cassell), page 8.
[36] Bloch, M. 1992. *Prey into Hunter* (Cambridge: Cambridge University Press).
[37] J. L. Austin. 1961. *Philosophical Papers* (Oxford: Clarendon).
[38] In part at least, Jesus' word to the potential disciple "Let the dead bury their dead" (Matt 8.22) is a reminder that we cannot live in the past. Life is the concrete now with all its changes, not the static past.

However this may be, Littlewood in reporting the work of other workers in the field of social anthropology notes their findings that ritual behaviour is not always an effective mediator of healing and wholeness. Where tensions exist in the social group, the rite may express these without necessarily offering any resolution (Littlewood: 22). Indeed, another social anthropologist goes further. She believes that rituals are only helpful where there exist relative social homogeneity and stasis, and expresses great pessimism about the ability of rituals to facilitate transition in any contemporary cultural context (Vizedom, 1976).

Despite Vizedom's pessimism, there is a widespread agreement that the disposal of the dead is not simply a public health matter. Whether people want to say "Goodbye" or give thanks for the life of the deceased, marking death by formal means still seems to have importance. The difficulty is to find ritual significance for that last act of compassion which gathers a group of mourners whom the liturgy addresses as a community.

The ritual community of death: gathering for the funeral

To speak of a ritual community or of a liturgical community is to invoke Vizedom's comment that effective ritual demands social cohesion. Not least of the contributing factors to the cohesion required in ritual and liturgy is shared belief. What has emerged in this chapter is that, although death has its impact on the social groupings to which the deceased belonged, there is no agreed body of belief about death. The privatisation of belief has led to the fragmentation of communal certainty, and its compartmentalisation has led to specialists who have sequestrated belief and ritual.[39] Among those specialists are ministers and clergy.

Tony Walter's call for funeral officiants to give to families the planning of the funeral might be understood superficially as a reaction against the specialist; but he does not make that connection. Indeed, Walter suggests that a "free market" approach to funeral arrangements might lead to the emergence of a group of clergy specialists whose expertise was acknowledged: "because they are good at funerals, not because they are hopeless at everything else!"[40]

Walter does not apparently intend to tackle the root problem for those who are asked to officiate at Christian funeral rite; his book primarily addresses the bereaved.[41] He has

---

[39] Sennett argues this in Part Four of *The Fall of Public Man*, "The Intimate Society" (pages 259-340). See also Mellor and Schilling, "Modernity, Self-Identity and the Sequestration of death", *Sociology*, vol. 27 (1993).

[40] The comment was made to Walter by a funeral director, but Walter cites it with apparent approval. The expression "free market" is mine, not Walter's, although I think it accurately reflects what he advocates.

[41] Although much of what Walter says forms a critique of funeral practice and so offers a direct commentary on the attitudes and activities of funeral directors and clergy, he writes from the perspective of his own experience of bereavement. His concern is to empower the bereaved. In the course of his proposals he does not always give consideration to the practicalities which Maura Naylor noted in her doctoral thesis for the University of Leeds, "The Funeral: The Management of Death and its Rituals in a Northern Industrial City", Department of Social Policy and Sociology, June 1989. The result is that, while his critique is one to which clergy and funeral directors should attend, Walter may be open to the suggestion that he has not seen the difficulties "from the other side of the counter".

much to say to those entrusted with many of the practicalities of funerals, but his critical stance does not address the question of the ritual community in a fragmented society. One of the tasks confronting the ritual president is to form a community for the rite. To this end (s)he will listen to the stories of the dead person as they are told by the bereaved.

If (s)he were to ask "What does this death mean?", there is no guarantee that any answer would be forthcoming. Of course, the question about meaning may be precisely the one which the bereaved themselves are asking – especially in those cases where a child has died or where death has been otherwise premature or violent. It may be that the officiant can in such circumstances build a community on the foundation of the shared question. If this question can be addressed to the God who has been bereaved, then there may be a way forward.[42] But many funerals are of the old who have suffered. For them death is a release, and the question uppermost in the minds of the bereaved is not what the death means but "Why did (s)he have to suffer?" While this is an important question, it may divert attention from the question about death – without which there would be no funeral.

For the vast majority of mourners death is dreadful because no meaning can be attached to it. In such circumstances the minister may open the order of service, and read "I am the resurrection and the life" with little confidence that the funeral is going to be a Christian rite in anything other than the words. The idea of a ritual community is empty.

Where death has no meaning beyond its finality, where it is a dead end, there can be no Christian rite of passage for the deceased. The journey for the deceased needs to place the dead in the world of the dead, but in Christian theology the world of the dead is not a world of non-being. The words of Jesus

> And as for the resurrection of the dead, have you not read what was said to you by God, 'I am the God of Abraham, the God of Isaac, and the God of Jacob'? He is God not of the dead, but of the living. (Matt 22.31 32)

challenge those who consign the dead to non-existence. This call reminds us that the rite of passage takes the dead person into a new world. There is a real passage into another mode of existence, and that existence is one of life.

The insistence of Jesus that the resurrection is a reality gives the Christian liturgist reason to examine carefully the work of van Gennep. Social anthropologists will themselves be divided in their reactions to the religious conviction of Jesus. However, their work on rites of passage provides an invaluable tool in enabling the funeral officiant to shape the liturgy not only for the bereaved, but also for the deceased. What draws the ritual community together at a funeral is death.

The funeral is for the dead person, and the mourners meet to say farewell. There is, therefore, the pastoral task of entrusting the mourners to God and of incorporating them

---

[42]   I have personal experience of such a way of proceeding in the funeral of a child. Not all the mourners had any formal religious belief, but the possibility of asking the question out loud, without soothing answers, led to an intensely moving experience in which all the anger and loss were shared and acknowledged. The family told the undertaker later that the funeral had been better for its honesty.

into the activity of God in Christ. Yet the Christian minister will surely want to enlarge that purpose. There is the primary ritual task of committing the dead to God, and of entrusting the dead to the Christ who himself died.

The dead person is placed at the centre of the rite, and the bereaved gather round.

CHAPTER 6

The Human in Christ

Introduction

The title of this chapter is deliberately ambiguous: it refers both to the humanity of Christ (Jesus the man) and to the new humanity in Christ (the redeemed). For the Christian theologian a description of what it means to be a person which is simply a "naming of parts" is inadequate. This is not just because in some way the whole is greater than the sum of its parts, but because the Christian does not see personhood in terms of atomic analysis. We exist both in relationship to one another and in relationship to God. These are creation categories of existence. Male and female are two parts of the one, but the myth of Adam and Eve gives assent to the further proposition that all humanity is related to its source and hence is "family". The answer to Cain's question "Am I my brother's keeper?" (Gen 4.9) is "Yes". Moreover, we rely upon God for breath itself (Gen 2.7) and are accountable to God for our living (Gen 3.8f.).

Further, the doctrine of the Incarnation ties God to the creation in such a way that the 'material' cannot be separated from the 'spiritual' in some Gnostic fashion. This insight had profound implications in the early development of Christian doctrine as it related both to the person of Christ and to salvation. Although the Two Nature theory made the unity of Christ's personhood susceptible to division, the Early Church resisted the challenge of dualism. The creation was not seen as the action of a Demiurge, and the salvation of the world was not achieved by a divided Christ – "What Christ has not assumed he has not healed". Nonetheless, the body-soul anthropology led to some extreme awkwardness of expression, as for example in the aphorism *apathos epathen* ("without suffering, he suffered").

I have suggested earlier that the Christian theologian is prompted to say more about what it means to be a human being, and that body-soul language is no longer an appropriate way of speaking. I have also suggested that a way forward may be to use the language of *nephesh*, *bios* and *zoe*. It is to this discussion that I wish shortly to turn after commenting upon one other matter.

For the Christian the life, and death and resurrection of Jesus are constitutive of what it means to live, to die and to be raised by God. It is central to the Christian tradition that we live and die in dependence upon and in relation to God, and that resurrection is God's answer to death. Such living, dying and resurrection is seen most completely in Jesus. It is therefore the task of this chapter to investigate a theological anthropology which will establish Jesus as normative for all human experience.[1]

My first task will be to look at a general anthropology and then to show how this is pre-eminently true for Jesus, and derivatively so for humanity in Christ. I shall then

---

[1] That is, the life, and death and resurrection of Jesus are what God normally intends for human beings. Our fallen nature frustrates this normality, and it is this that makes essential the doctrine of the atonement.

argue that the death and resurrection of Christ are representative in their function, and that the salvation offered in the Paschal Mystery offers hope not only for the living but for the dead. Finally, I shall indicate how these considerations raise questions for our understanding of what a funeral is meant to do.

Personal anthropology: *nephesh*, death and resurrection

In the Old Testament, *nephesh* is a way of describing the living being, and one of its most common uses is reflexive ("I will do this myself"). *Nephesh* is not simply a category of description reserved for humans or even for created beings.[2] When Yahweh speaks to Moses in Leviticus there are examples of *nephesh* being used in this reflexive way, and a similar usage occurs in the Book of Psalms.[3] Frequently *nephesh* has been translated as 'soul', but it may also be rendered 'self'.[4]

Thinking of *nephesh* as the self is a useful point of departure for the anthropology that I wish to propose. A human person is an ordered self. This ordering is effected by God's breathing into us and by social relationships as well as by centred conscious awareness. I gain knowledge of who I am by my own self-awareness, by the awareness and recognition which others accord to me, and by the awareness and recognition granted to me by God.

These external identifications are important. They confirm who I am when I cannot identify myself.[5] At its most trivial and commonplace this recognition may be accorded to me when I am asleep. More seriously, it may be granted to me when I am in a trauma – of either a physiological or psychological kind.

I am still me, even if I have lost arms and legs or have collapsed after an accident or surgical operation into a coma. I am equally still me if I have lost all recognition of who I am. The 'me' in such a trauma is obviously in some sense diminished, but I remain the one whom God called into being and whose history makes me who I am. This also holds true in the realm of human development. In the early stages there is a growing self-awareness; yet before the infant 'I' knows who I am, I am known by others.

This external recognition tells against those who end up by giving my psychological history a distinct ontology from 'me'. Even though those who recognise me may only do so with difficulty, even though they may say "He's not himself any longer" or "He's not who he was", there is yet the recognition that the 'he' of whom they speak is related to the previous 'he' whom they remember as me. There is change and alteration; but there is also continuity.

Of course, the human person is not only accorded recognition by others. In relationship with others there is formation and growth into personhood. Our personhood is ordered by its self-awareness, its relationship to others and its calling into existence

---

[2]   For example, in Lev 24.18 *nephesh* is used of an animal.

[3]   Lev 26.11, 13; Ps 11.5. Yahweh has, or is, a *nephesh*!

[4]   There are many other translations: mind, heart, life, one, someone, body or corpse, appetite, desire or throat, breath, lust, person, will.

[5]   They are not, however, exclusive or incontrovertibly accurate or complete. My own self-awareness is not necessarily false.

by God. This ordered being I refer to as the *nephesh*. However distorted or diminished it may become, the *nephesh* is the self.

Bios is that which the *nephesh* organises in order to be a living being. If the *nephesh*, as we at present experience it, is embodied, then *bios* is the energy which *nephesh* embodies. This *bios* may be thought of as the breath which made Adam from the dust. In everyday speech it is 'life'. When in everyday speech we talk of being alive, it is with *bios* that we are concerned. The important thing to observe here is that this language does not separate *bios* from the religious or spiritual sphere. *Bios* is the gift of God; and this way of speaking reminds us that our everyday living is dependent upon God. All life is given, and cannot be compartmentalised into those areas which belong to God and those which do not.

Zoe is our response to the call by God to live teleologically. It is not separate from *bios*, nor is *bios* separate from *zoe*. *Zoe* is the God-ward orientation of *bios*; it is *bios* lived to a "zoetic" end. To live in a zoetic way is to live with a *nephesh* in which *bios* and *zoe* are in harmony. Sin is both the failure to order *bios* zoetically and the state in which that failure occurs. Just as *bios* is inclusive of all our living, so also is *zoe*. There are no areas of existence which fall outside the teleological purposes of God.

To summarise, the *nephesh* is the way in which *bios* is organised, and this organisation is both individual and social. A *nephesh* which organises that God-given *bios* to fulfil the purposes of God expresses itself in *zoe*. By speaking in this way, we avoid a dualism which allows the body to decay in death while asserting that an immortal soul escapes. And it is to death that we now must turn.

Whatever model we used to describe human existence, no amount of argument can disguise the fact that we die. Indeed, Heidegger described human existence as being-unto-death. For the theological position I am arguing, death is a total event. Nothing escapes. As Barth comments: "When we die, all things and we ourselves come to an end" (Barth, 1960a: 588).

Karl Rahner sees the resurrection of the body and the immortality of the soul as parallel statements arising from different ways of speaking of the human (Rahner: 352). He is unwilling to allow that death can be adequately described as separation of soul and body (Rahner: 127), and writes later that "death puts an end to the *whole* man" (Rahner: 347).[6]

The totality of death is a crucial tenet to the theological understanding I am pursuing. Like Rahner, I cannot subscribe to a dualist description of death. Since I want to describe human personhood and life in unitary terms, I am committed to a similar stance in relation to death. When we die our *bios* seeps away and our *nephesh* loses its organisational control.[7] Such an understanding is harmonious with the findings of medical science; and while I do not want to grant to medicine a metaphysical competence, a theology of death which ignores what we know of *bios* is to my mind perverse. Since my life in response to God's calling (*zoe*) is given to me as a *nephesh*, it too ceases – with neither *nephesh* nor *bios*. Insofar as *zoe* is a response to the calling of

---

6   The stress is Rahner's.

7   The dead are described as *rephaim* (powerless shades) in the Old Testament. This corresponds to my description of a *nephesh* losing *bios* (energy).

God, it too ceases to exist. On the other hand, the *telos*, to which we are called by God, continues independently of the existence of those who are summoned to its consummation, for the *telos* is the eternal purpose of God.

Resurrection is, then, a gracious act of God in which *bios* and *zoe* are restored to a re-ordered *nephesh*. The *nephesh* is differently organised beyond death. If we speak of an embodiment, a resurrection of the body, then that body will be the "spiritual body" of which St Paul speaks in 1 Corinthians 15. Resurrection is a new creation in which the energy (*bios*), which the *nephesh* organised before death in embodied form, is now reconstituted and organised in the *nephesh* beyond death. The *zoe* of God, our life in response to God's teleological claim, is (by God's word of resurrection) lived by the *nephesh* in freedom. Resurrection is not simply the same old thing beyond death. It is life in a radically new dimension of eschatological liberty.[8] Rahner puts it thus:

> We do not mean that 'things go on' after death, as though we only changed horses, as Feuerbach puts it, and rode on . . .
>
> Eternity is not an immeasurably long-lasting mode of pure time, but a mode of the spirit and freedom . . . (Rahner: 347, 348)

The importance of such an understanding of death and resurrection for funeral liturgies lies in the challenge it brings to the body-soul anthropology which is so commonly assumed. Language which speaks of commending the soul to God and committing the body to the elements loses its place. The whole person is dead, and the whole person must be relinquished to God. Resurrection is different from immortality, and the anthropology which I propose affirms resurrection as an act of God in response to the totality of death.

However, there is a further liturgical consideration. A growing emphasis is being placed on the idea that the funeral service should be a celebration of the Paschal Mystery. The significance of this emphasis is that it addresses the transcendental questions about God which death poses. It is, therefore, to the life, death and resurrection of Jesus that I now wish to apply the theological anthropology of *nephesh*, *bios* and *zoe*.

Jesus as normative

I have already indicated that I have reservations about the Two Nature theory. If, as I have argued, human nature may be described satisfactorily in terms of relationship to God without recourse to our body-soul anthropology, then the Two Nature theory is not necessary for the construction of a Christology. Jesus was a *nephesh*; his uniqueness

---

[8]   Young, F. 1990. *Face to Face: A narrative essay in the theology of suffering* (Edinburgh: T. & T. Clark). Frances Young tells the story of her handicapped son Arthur and reflects as mother and theologian on what Arthur's experience means for our understanding both of personhood and of God. She concludes that resurrection cannot mean a "making perfect" which would erase both the suffering and joy of Arthur's life by making him "normal". To deny his handicapped experience in such a way would be to suggest that his life is sub-human. Professor Young has no easy answer to the questions about the darkness of God. The intellectual rigour she applies to her family life is profoundly moving. I believe that my anthropology is open to what she has written; I would certainly want it no other way.

consists in his ability to harmonise *bios* and *zoe*. "He was obedient", runs the *carmen Christi*; "Son though he was he learnt obedience" declares the writer of the letter to the Hebrews.[9] It is in this obedience to God that he demonstrates normative humanity in which *zoe* and *bios* are one. This is what it means to be normatively human: to live life in obedience to the calling of God.

The death of Jesus exemplifies his loving obedience of God. This is the thrust both of the *carmen Christi* and of the reference in Hebrews. When Jesus gives up his spirit (Lk 23.46), it is the breath (*pneuma*) that has given life (*bios*) to his *nephesh* that he returns to God. The docetic hypothesis that Jesus' death is incomplete (or even feigned) is impossible in my reading, since the suggestion depends upon the Two Nature theory.

The death of Jesus is total, as is our death. The sense of abandonment which Jesus feels is a recognition that death is "a return to non-being".[10] The dead go down to Sheol where there is no praise of God, no communion with the source of all life that calls us into being. To this I shall shortly return, for Jesus' descent to the dead is a crucial sign of hope in which the death of death is worked.

The resurrection of Jesus is the mighty act of God in which the *bios* of Jesus is reconstituted and finds itself newly organised in a resurrection *nephesh*. The *zoe* of Jesus results in the bringing to glory of the children of God. This is accomplished in the ministry he exercised in life and in death, and which by the resurrection he exercises yet. This resurrection is the expression of Christian hope for the creation, which groans for its freedom (Rom 8.19-25). This ministry, too, is normative.

When we speak of the dead at the funeral, we speak by reference to Christ the firstborn from the dead (Col 1.17). The funeral rite which fails to make this connection is, in my judgement, inadequately Christian. It fails to establish Christ as our representative. There is a cosmic implication to the descent of Christ to the dead which ought to be expressed in the funeral liturgy.

I intend to address myself in the remainder of this chapter to this universal reference of Christ's death. I shall do so first by a consideration of this teaching as it occurs in 1 Peter and in Origen's later development. At the conclusion of the chapter I shall show how the theologian, Dorothee Sölle, working in the second half of the twentieth century, expounded a theory of Christ as representative.

Holy Saturday and the descent to the dead[11]

If, as I have argued, the death of Jesus is so complete that he is incapable of any activity, then it follows that the descent to the dead belongs to the realm of myth. A meta-historical event is being described in terms which demand of us a theological rather than an historical response.

The Apostles' Creed says simply "he descended into hell". The Greek has *eis Haidou* – "into (the realm) of Hades", and we might wish to avoid the confusion about

---

9   Phil 2.8; Heb 5.8.
10 Barth describes death in this way when he speaks of death as a sign of judgement (1960a: 595ff).
11 See also, Sheppy, P. P. J. 1997. "Towards a theology of transition", in P. C. Jupp and A. Rogers (eds.), *Interpreting Death: Christian theology and pastoral practice* (London: Cassell).

the nature of hell as a place of punishment by translating this clause "he descended to [the realm of] the dead".

The language of descent ought not be understood in spatial terms. "He descended to the dead" is simply a way of saying "he died". Nonetheless, the metaphor of descent is hospitable to a theology which wants to say that in Jesus' death there was a progress to God which was inclusive of all the dead. The scriptural warrant for this clause is the passage in 1 Peter running from 3.18 to 4.6.

The question which all students of that text must decide is: Who are the "imprisoned spirits"? Church Fathers and modern New Testament scholars have proposed various possibilities, and it may be helpful to summarise the main lines of argument here.

1. *The reference is to Noah's contemporaries.*
    In this case, verse 20 makes a very natural contrast between the obedient Noah and the disobedient people of his day – a contrast that was frequently made in Jewish teaching of the period and by Jesus himself. The internal textual support for this understanding is provided by 4.6 where *nekrois* is used rather than *pneumasin*. In 3.19, *pneumata* is used to describe the souls of the dead. The passage speaks of a proclamation to the dead.

2. *They are the spirits of the fallen angels to which Gen 6.2-4 refers.*
    These were the subject of a great deal of speculation in contemporary Jewish apocalyptic. It was a major theme in the Book of Enoch, which describes these "spirits" as being in Gehenna or the abyss.

3. *Jesus' proclamation is to the "righteous dead" of Israel.*
    This view is a qualification of (1) and takes the view that 1 Peter is a conservative text, which is unlikely to be advocating a universalist soteriology. The understanding of *pneumata* as the dead is once more contested. J. R. Michaels rejects *phulakē* as meaning "a prison", and prefers to translate "security" (Michaels: 205-211, 234-242). In advocating this view, Michaels urges us to understand the preaching to the dead, referred to in 4.6, as preaching in their lifetime. The link between 3.19 and 4.6 is severed, and the writer is understood to be rehearsing God's covenant-faithfulness to those who heard the good news before Christ and repented in their day. In this way the story of Noah is accommodated.

The second understanding (a reference to the fallen angels) is frequently favoured for two main reasons.

1. Pneumata *is very infrequently used of those who have died.*
    For such an idea, the usual Greek word is *psychai*. There are instances of *pneumata* being used for "the dead", but they are rare.

2. *The passage 3.18-22 ends with the exaltation of Christ over all the spiritual powers.*
    In such a setting (3.19), *ekēryxen* could scarcely be a proclamation of the gospel. Rather, "made proclamation" would refer to the exaltation and sovereignty of Jesus (3.22), whose suffering was according to the flesh (4.1) and whose exaltation was to God. This theme is found elsewhere in

the New Testament. On such a view *en phulakē* (3.19) must mean that the *pneumata* are guarded, but not necessarily "underground". Indeed, the suggestion is that they are in the heavenly realms and that the risen Christ makes the proclamation after his exaltation and ascension.

Against this view, we should note that:

– 3.18-22 needs to be read within the context to 4.6.

– It is still not finally demonstrated beyond argument that the *pneumata* are not those of the dead.

– It would then follow that *kēryssein* (3.19) might be understood in its normal New Testament usage as a synonym for *euangelizesthai* (4.6).

This line of argument observes the link with 4.6 very closely. Indeed, the cited example of Noah is given specific force since the people of the Flood were, in Jewish thought, the wickedest people of all time and for them there simply was no hope. The reference here to the selfsame people suggests that, contrary to conventional religious wisdom, those with no hope can find hope since Christ himself has brought it to them. This exegesis is lent force by the echo of Jesus' warning that the inhabitants of Sodom and Gomorrah would find hope in the judgement before those who heard his proclamation and refused it (Matt 10.13-15; 11. 20-24).

Against the view held by Michaels, that Jesus' proclamation is to the righteous dead of Israel, we may argue that:

– The universalist line of interpretation of this text began in the early church with Irenaeus and Origen (whose understanding of Greek and its nuances was presumably at least as good as our own). They were able to read the passage in the context of "conservative" 1 Peter and to place upon it a wider soteriology without embarrassment – though, of course, not without theological controversy!

– To propose that 4.6 is written simply to remind its readers that God keeps covenant-faithfulness with those repentant before Jesus requires that it be held apart from 3.19-22. The point can easily be made without any reference to the descent of Jesus *eis Haidou*. Such a separation is, in my judgement, forced and I stand by my earlier comments.

Leonhard Goppelt, in his commentary on 1 Peter, takes a similar view and sides with those who see the text as a *kērygma* to the dead. He writes:

"The spirits in prison" are, therefore, the souls of the flood generation preserved in a place of punishment after death. 1 Peter 3:19 f. contains, therefore, an important kerygmatic statement. In rabbinic tradition the generation of the Flood were regarded as thoroughly and ultimately lost: "The generation of the Flood have no share in the world to come".[12] But 1 Peter declares: Even to this most lost part of humanity Christ, the One who died and rose, offers salvation (Goppelt: 259).

---

[12]   *M. Sanhedrin* 10:3a, *The Mishnah*, transl. H. Danby (1958: 397).

Pannenberg sketches the doctrinal implications arising from such a position in his book on the Apostles' Creed (Pannenberg, 1972: 90-95). After remarking that the clause "he descended" was a later insertion into the Roman baptismal creed, Pannenberg suggests that the rejection by God's people which Jesus experienced in his death would have implied rejection by God himself. Hell is to be understood as conscious separation from God of creatures who are utterly dependent upon the gifts of God for existence and sustenance.

Yet even this is not enough; for the Church has historically held another theology of the descent into hell, seeing it not in terms of Christ's suffering but of his triumph over death and hell (cf. Eph 4.8-10;[13] Col 1.18-20). The universalist tendency of the 1 Peter text was bold even for the Early Church. Only in the face of considerable controversy was Origen able to develop this idea and to talk of the redemption of Adam. Later, the harrowing of hell became a prominent theme of Christian art – both in the mystery plays and in painting.

As the tradition of the Early Church about the descent to the dead developed, it found its most radical expositor in Origen for whose theology it had a great soteriological importance. He asked the very questions which the funeral officiant is forced to ask. "Who is to be saved?" "Is the gospel good news only for a few or for all?" "Is there hope for the dead?" His answers depended upon his understanding of the immortality of the soul and upon his doctrine of the resurrection of the body. Such beliefs were readily available to his contemporaries; where he begins to break new ground is in his perception that the descent and proclamation to the dead place salvation in a universal context.

As the expectation of an imminent parousia of Christ in glory faded, first martyrdom and then monasticism became exemplars of Christian life here on earth. With this change in emphasis, the question of death and what lay beyond assumed greater theological importance. The earlier Pauline timescale which provided for those still alive at the parousia was long since irrelevant. Piety and devotion may have called Christians to be ready for the Lord's imminent return, but the reality was that it was their own death that was now seen as the gateway to the eternal presence of God. Into the vacuum of experimental evidence theology poured speculation and theory; it could do little else.[14]

---

[13] I acknowledge that not all exegetes understand *ta katōtera tēs gēs* as a reference to Christ's descent to hell. Caird (1976:73ff.), for example, prefers to understand the passage as a reference to the outpouring of gifts at Pentecost.

[14] This is not to suggest that in some way Christian believing lost a hypothetical "original purity". We do well to remember J. N. D. Kelly's comment:

> It is not infrequently alleged that after the first generation Christianity underwent a radical transformation. The assurance of living in the Messianic age and enjoying the first-fruits of the Spirit, so powerfully evident in the Epistles, is held to have yielded place to the conception of God's kingdom of the region or state, located exclusively in the future, which is reserved as a prize for those who have struggled manfully in this life . . . Nevertheless, it is misleading to concentrate on such one-sided expressions of the Christian faith. In the early centuries, as indeed in other epochs, wherever religion was alive and healthy, the primitive conviction of enjoying already the benefits of the age to come was kept vividly before the believer's consciousness . . . True enough, the resurrection and judgement, along with the Saviour's second coming, lay ahead

Justin Martyr and Athenagoras[15] were among the first to offer a reasoned apologetic for the doctrine of the resurrection. Justin refuted the apparent impossibility of the idea by denying that the matter was beyond God's ability. He argued that if human sperm could be transformed into flesh and bones, then (by analogy) the dead could most certainly be transformed into resurrection life (*1 Apol.*, 18). Athenagoras reaffirmed God's intention and power to raise the dead. He began by rebutting suggestions that the resurrection was impossible because of the variety of fates which befell the human body.[16] He then argued for the resurrection on two main grounds: the nature of what it is to be human, and the purposes of God.

For Athenagoras, human nature "is constituted by an immortal soul and the body which has been united with it at its creation" (*de Res.*, 15.2). Although Athenagoras is urgent in arguing for a psychosomatic unity, he does so from a different starting point from the Hebraic notion of *nephesh*. Here we are in contact with the writer whose purpose is to address not a Hebraic but a Hellenistic readership and audience. The Platonist conception of the immortal soul gives a different rationale for the teaching of resurrection. Since the soul is immortal and human nature demands an accompanying body, the body must be raised. Human nature manifests its concern for the future beyond death in the desire for children who will be a heritage:

> He also begets children, not for his own use nor for the sake of anything else about which he is concerned, but that his offspring may continue in existence as long as possible, thus consoling himself for his own death by a succession of children and descendants and in this way thinking to make the mortal immortal (*de Res.*, 12.2).

Thus the ground for belief in the resurrection of the body is in the affections of the immortal soul. Although this might appear to be a vague yearning without any grounding in reality, Athenagoras was able to assume the immortality of the soul as a philosophical *datum* for those to whom he wrote. The action of God in raising the body was linked to the question of theodicy. The omissions and errors of human justice and the chances and circumstances of this life must be put right (*de Res.*, 18.2-19.7), and this requires the survival of the body with which the immortal soul was united at creation (*de Res.*, 20.3).

For Irenaeus, the eschatological concern was to emphasise the importance of the body against the Gnostic doctrine of the soul's superiority to the body as "gold in the mud".[17] Gnostic teaching understood salvation as a great escape in which the spiritual[18]

---

in the temporal future. But already, through baptism, the faithful catechumen participated in the resurrection; he had died and risen again with Christ, and now lived the life of the Spirit. (1965: 460, 461).

[15] The doubts about Athenagoras' authorship of *de Resurrectione* were thoroughly explored by R. M. Grant nearly fifty years ago, but here I shall observe the traditional attribution.

[16] Not simply its disintegration, but the dismemberment of bodies before and after death – including the eating of the body by animals.

[17] Irenaeus was not alone in this controversy; Tertullian and Hippolytus also offered an orthodox defence against the thrust of Gnosticism.

[18] Not every human soul was seen as *pneumatikos*; salvation was inevitably the preserve of an elite.

soul at last eluded the clutches of the earthly and material, and returned to the *plērōma*.[19] Irenaeus argued that God was indeed the Creator of the material world. Not only could God raise the body to life, it was necessary that God should do so. The body is subject to the *Logos* of God, and our salvation is effective for all that we are – body and soul (*adv. Haer.*, 5.2.2; 5.3.2; 5.20.1). Above all, however, the importance of the body and therefore the greatest evidence of the resurrection is shown by the incarnation. If the *Logos* became flesh, he could only have done so in order to save human flesh (*adv. Haer.*, 5.12; 5.13.1).

Yet it is with Origen that we come to writings that express a development from the apologetic to the "systematic", for it is Origen who uses the work of his predecessors to attempt a coherent philosophical theology.[20] Working with the tools of Platonism, Origen assumes the immortality of the soul. Human souls are spirits fallen from a pre-existent, invisible world;[21] salvation is the restoration (*apokatastasis*) of all things[22] to this earliest state (cf. 1 Cor 15.23-28).

Death is the common lot of all humans (as of all animals), and as a natural event it is an occurrence without value. However, death may also be experienced as either "death to sin " or "death in sin". These are respectively good and evil in their relation to the soul. The former is what St Paul talks of in Romans 6 – the Christ-like death which leads to sharing in his resurrection; the latter is opposition to the divine life of the Spirit. "Common death" is the separation of the soul from the body.

In the *Dialogue with Heraclides* Origen concludes that the principal argument for the immortality of the soul is the need for divine justice. In *de Principiis* he supplements this line, in effect rehearsing the arguments of Athenagoras in *de Resurrectione*. However, he also introduces the Platonist idea of "participation" in which all earthly things share in the corresponding heavenly realities (*de Princ.*, 4.4.9-10). Human souls and angelic beings participate to differing degrees in a common reality – namely, immortality and incorruptibility. Further, since every being that has life draws it from God, all must share in the immortality of God.

This last idea is a subtle (and powerful) advance on other arguments for the immortality of the soul. Hitherto (although the distinction would have been meaningless to Origen and his predecessors), the immortality of the soul seems to have been thought of as innate – rather than the act of grace which the writers of the biblical material believed the resurrection to be. Here, however, it may be that we move toward a notion that immortality is itself an act of grace in creation, as God in some sense imparts

---

[19]   Gnosticism was not all of a piece, and there were varying shades and nuances of the doctrine – as with any great religious tradition. Nonetheless, the summary given here may, I think, be fairly regarded as a useful composite précis.

[20]   Von Campenhausen (1963: 474) writes of Origen that "he was the only one [of the Greek Fathers] to present the whole of Christianity in the form of a workable philosophical system".

[21]   In *de Principiis* (2.9.3-4) Origen suggests that this fall entailed a cooling (*psychesthai*) and proposes that the *psychē* is so called because of this *psychesthai*. As people are more or less open to the dying, so they reveal the greater or lesser cooling of their souls.

[22]   J. N. D. Kelly (1965: 474) believes that Origen is ambivalent on this point. At times, the purgative fire of judgement is apparently able to restore even the devil to grace (*de Princ.*, 3.6.5); at other times, the unrepentant sinner is beyond such hope (cf. *Comm. Jn.*, 19.14(3),88)

himself to the soul. Platonist categories of thought, which were for Origen his native philosophical air, probably inhibited any further accommodation of Hebraic ideas of resurrection. For Origen, the resurrection of the body was a means to an end in a way which the biblical use of the idea could never be. For Paul, and the other canonical witnesses to the resurrection of the body, it was the end *per se*.

When the body is seen only as the vehicle for the soul, its resurrection is dependent (if it is deemed necessary) upon the soul's immortality being transferred to it by association or by an act which is undertaken solely to meet the soul's needs. Where, however, the human personality is a genuine unity (rather than an association of unequal partners), resurrection is of that unity which makes up the totality of human existence. The biblical *corpus* is a collection of Jewish writings using predominantly Jewish traditions and thought forms. The emphasis is quite distinct from that of Greek Platonism.

Yet Origen gave great weight to the resurrection of the body and rejected Gnostic spirituality which allowed no place for the body in the experience of salvation after death. He was aware of the way in which critics attempted to laugh the idea out of court, and he rejected the crudest literal views which assigned to post-resurrection bodies those functions for which there would be no use after death.

The question arises as to whether a body so changed can be recognisably the same body; and, if not, how the purpose for which Origen argued for its resurrection could be met. If the body is so changed that it is no longer the same, how can the issues of reward and punishment in the final judgment be adequately met?

Origen begins by noting how even in this life our bodies change while we still remain recognisable (*Comm. Ps. 1*).[23] He then distinguishes between the underlying level of matter (*to hylikon hypokeimenon*) – at which fluidity and changeability occur – and the characteristic form (*to charaktērizon eidos*) where continuity is to be found. At the resurrection the *eidos* will be recognisably the same, whereas the qualities of the *hylikon hypokeimenon* will be adapted to heavenly rather than earthly needs and circumstances.

Methodius, to whom we owe our fragmentary knowledge of this argument from his citation of Origen in *Aglaophon*, mistook Origen's use of the term for *eidos* and interpreted it as having the popular sense of external appearance. He then suggested that what Origen was really teaching was that in the resurrection we receive a different (glorious) body which has the same outward appearance as our old earthly one. In fact, Origen was concerned to preserve a real identity between the earthly and glorious bodies and he used *eidos* for precisely that reason.[24]

In his consideration of the death and resurrection of Christ, Origen offers a number of different theories of the redemption: Christ pays the debt for our sins, nailing the bond to the cross (cf. Col 2.14); Christ overcomes the devil and parades the defeated

---

[23] There is between the earthly body and its resurrection counterpart both resemblance and similarity, and elsewhere Origen refers to the analogy that St Paul made in 1 Corinthians 15 to a seed and the plant it produces.

[24] Henri Crouzel (1989: 248-257) describes in great detail Origen's doctrine of the resurrection of the body and its misinterpretation by both Methodius and Epiphanius.

forces of evil (cf. Col 2.15); Christ incorporates us in our baptism as we share in his death and resurrection (cf. Rom 6.3-11); Christ offers himself in a sin-offering as both priest and victim (echoing the priestly theology of the Epistle to the Hebrews); Christ pays the price (according to Origen, to the devil) for our liberation (cf. 1 Pet 1.18-19; Rev 5.9).

It is in this last image that we find the morally awkward idea of God pulling the wool over the devil's eyes. If the purchase is to be real, then the payment (Christ) cannot really be recovered. In order to meet this objection, Origen proposes that all the devil takes into Hades is Christ's soul without being aware that this soul is united with the eternal *Logos*. The devil is thus tricked into "selling" enslaved humanity back to God, since only a pure soul can understand the ways of God and the devil has no such understanding.[25] God keeps the redeemed; and Christ's soul, united with the *Logos*, remains free.

In constructing his theology of salvation, Origen pays considerable attention to the descent to the dead. Hades (by which name Origen refers to Sheol, which he distinguishes from Gehenna – the eternal fire) is the region of the dead where, following the sins of Adam which closed the gates of Paradise, God's Old Testament saints await Christ's passion and descent. Christ's descent to Hades reverses the devil's captivity of humanity:

> After having vanquished the demons, his enemies, Christ led the people, who were under their sway, as if these people were the booty of victory and the spoils of salvation (*Hom. Num.*, 18.4).

Here is an echo of Eph 4.8:

> He ascended into the heights;
> he took captives into captivity;
> he gave gifts to men.

Hades is closed for ever; the faithful may enter Paradise through the now-open gates.

Origen is sensitive to the Gnostic charge that eternal punishment is unfitting for a "spiritual" God, and reflects Old Testament rather than New Testament images. He therefore spiritualises the fire of Gehenna and sees its "food and material" as the wood, straw and stubble to which St Paul refers in 1 Corinthians 3. In so doing, he draws on Stoic ideas in which the "passions" are compared with a burning fever. It is in this connection that he develops his doctrine of *apokatastasis*.

In fact, as Crouzel notes (Crouzel: 257), Origen rarely uses either the noun or its cognate verb, and he does not regard his teaching as anything new. Indeed, he views his work as an explication of the Pauline doctrine of 1 Cor 15.25.

---

[25] In his own terms, Origen escapes the moral difficulty by his insistence that only the pure soul can know and understand the ways of God. While we may still remain dissatisfied with a transaction of false balances, Origen did not see the contract as one between equals. For our own moral sensibilities no other transaction can be honest, and a redemption based on a dishonesty is unworthy of God and unworkable in integrity. To say all this, however, may be no more than to say that we cannot ourselves use this particular theory of Origen's; it does not necessarily subvert the theory in its proponent's terms.

It is often suggested that in *de Principiis* Origen suggests that the devil will share in the final restoration (*de Princ.*, 3.6.5). Yet the passage in question refers to death rather than to the devil. While elsewhere death and the devil are linked as the final enemy and represent a denial of all that God is, in this context there is no such explicit link made. In a later text, the *Letter to Friends in Alexandria*, Origen records that he is alleged to believe in the salvation of the devil and forthrightly rejects such a view.

De Principiis is not to be taken as Origen's final statement, but as an interim stage in theological exploration. Earlier he had indeed questioned whether the demons could be converted (*de Princ.*, 1.6.2). The thesis was advanced that they might exercise their freedom of will in favour of goodness, for God could surely not have created them evil. However, this postulate did not end the journey for Origen. In his *Commentary on John* he describes how consistency of habit produces a human character or nature. This means security for the righteous who have become by frequent charity unchangeably free by nature; it also means that the demons (and, of course, the devil) make themselves evil by nature.

What happens to me when I die? For the faithful the fire of judgment awaits, yet its primary purpose is purification – a process which can begin in this life as the believer's thoughts and actions are purged by God. For those who have been mystically united with the death and resurrection of Christ in baptism, the hope is of restoration with and by God. As for the fate of the unrepentant, Origen hesitates to adopt an unqualified doctrine of eternal punishment – the objections of the Gnostics and his own philosophical conscience have too much force. The references in scripture and to eternal fire are very powerful, yet his personal hope for a universal *apokatastasis* is unremitting. In balancing the two, Origen returns to the concept of free will and has to allow that it must be possible for some (if freedom is to be true freedom) to reject the proffered restoration.

In reviewing (albeit briefly) Origen's teaching, we cannot claim that in the intervening centuries the essentials of the argument have much changed. Whatever our reaction to Origen's conclusions, he has laid out the main areas of debate.

For the dying, the descent of Jesus to the dead on Holy Saturday has two implications: that death is not alien to God, and that where we go alone Jesus himself has gone alone; and that even in our death and beyond our dying the cross of Christ has redemptive power.

Pastorally, the first implication means that in the mystery of death we encounter the greater mystery of God. The incarnation is completed in the darkness of death, and the theme "what Christ has not assumed he has not healed" gains a further dynamic. In our death we lose all that we own: our material possessions, our status, our achievements, our ambitions – even our self and identity. In this stripping we are left alone with nothing, and here we are confronted by the mystery of God who can take of that nothing and make a new creation. The Priestly account of creation in Genesis 1 talks of the creative spirit of God hovering over the deep. Out of that primeval chaos God creates *ex nihilo*.[26] In our dying and death, where the homeostasis of our bio-system disintegrates

---

[26] I do not understand creation *ex nihilo* as God producing previously non-existent matter out of thin air in the manner of a conjurer. Rather I take it to mean the producing of order, pattern and system out of chaos.

and deteriorates into chaos, God is at work once again in a new creation *ex nihilo*. We cannot know in what form we shall share in this new creation, and it is pastorally unwise to offer as certainty what can only ever be speculation. Our destiny is to live as Jesus lived, united to God by ties of perfect love. Herein is resurrection begun; herein is the death of death initiated. In the words of the Psalmist:

> darkness is not too dark for you and night is as light as day;
> to you both dark and light are one (Ps 139.12).

The second implication is yet more daring. While death is a "once for all" event beyond which lies judgement, judgement is not to be understood simply as the condemnation of those who have not during their earthly life professed faith in propositional terms which accord with our understanding of the gospel. In the mercy and grace of God, even the people of Sodom and Gomorrah are led out from the realm of the dead in Jesus' great victory parade. The universalist implications of the cross are suggested more forcefully here than perhaps much evangelism allows. The death of Jesus is the death of death, which no longer has power to separate the creation from the source of all life and love. The *tetelestai* from the cross is not simply the cry of a man who has accomplished what he has set out to do. It is the utterance of a pious Jew who means by "it is accomplished" no less than "God has brought to its goal the plan of salvation".[27] The descent to the dead is made in order to proclaim this gospel to those apparently otherwise without hope.

Christ the representative: the Paschal Mystery and human death

Jesus is often referred to as "the Man for Others". This may be variously taken to mean the one who offered himself in service to others, or the one who by his life and death offered himself to God for the world. It is this second emphasis which I want to examine. In particular I want to ask in what sense we can describe the death of Jesus as being "for us".

Evangelical theology has primarily espoused a substitutionary theory of the atonement in which Jesus is seen as dying in our place, instead of us. The problem for such a view is twofold and simply stated. Where is the morality in putting a guiltless person to a death which the guilty deserve? How can one man's death release all others from their deaths?

The answers traditionally given rely upon an appreciation of the awfulness of sin, the demand for a perfect sacrifice, and the idea that the sinlessness of the one will pay

---

(Of course, we ought to note in passing that the conjurer does not in fact produce things out of thin air!) Further, the doctrine of creation *ex nihilo* is designed to state the priority of the Creator to the creation, the distinction between the two, and the creation's dependence upon God for all its continuing existence.

[27]   Cf. Matt 7.7, where "it will be given you" and "it will be opened to you" are ways of describing how God answers the petitions of those who pray. The use of the impersonal third person singular is a typical instance of the Jewish reserve about pronouncing the name of God.

We ought also to note that *telos* and *tetelestai* are cognate. The cry from the cross indicates that God has in Christ brought *bios* and *zoe* into perfect (*teleios*!) unity.

for the sin of the many.[28] However powerfully these suggestions are made and however widespread their acceptance, there are those who feel that there is an unresolved moral dilemma in this theory.

The substitutionists point to the Marcan phrase "a ransom for many" (10.45), and rightly interpret the Greek preposition *anti* to mean "in place of". Yet the NT appearances of *anti* are overwhelmed by the incidence of *hyper*, which does not mean "in place of" but "on behalf of".[29] The NT emphasis is not on substitution but representation. For example, Paul's theology of being in Christ depends on representation rather than on substitution. It is not so much that Christ dies in my place so that I do not have to die, but that his death makes sense of and gives meaning and hope to mine. John Robinson argued this in his essay "What future for a unique Christ?" (Robinson, 1987: 9-17), but perhaps the most complete modern exposition has been Dorothee Sölle's *Christ the Representative*.

Such an understanding leads to a soteriological shift. Rather than seeing Jesus' death as objectively complete, the substitutionary view relies upon the believer to appropriate the death of Jesus for her/himself. Substitutionists deny this; but in my judgement their view leads us to see the death of Jesus as rather like a French railway ticket that needs validating before it can be used. The salvation afforded by the cross is limited by human response.

A representationist, however, may argue that the cross is complete in itself. The work has been done, regardless of human response. The weakness of this view, it may be urged, is that it denies to human beings their accountability before God. Yet a thoroughgoing representationist view may argue that Jesus has made the acceptable response to God on behalf of (*hyper*) all – that is, as their representative.[30]

---

[28] I can remember as a child hearing preachers use the illustration of a judge who imposes a fine that the guilty person is unable to pay (the lawful punishment). The judge then proceeds to pay from his own resources (the act of mercy). Even to the mind of a child this posed a problem: judges simply don't behave in this way! I was never able to discover an actual instance in which this had occurred. I was told that this was "just an illustration", but I knew that the picture was not true. Moreover, never when I heard the story was the punishment anything more than a fine. Even the preachers dared not suggest that a judge would go to prison – or, indeed, pay with his life! As St Paul remarks (Rom 5.8), God's love is beyond human parallel. We cannot make such an illustration.

[29] There are 13 instances of *anti* meaning "for" in the New Testament. Of *hyper*, meaning "on behalf of", there are 132 appearances.

[30] Sölle argues a completely contrary case to mine in distinguishing substitution from representation. She argues that it is substitution that eradicates human response, and representation that demands it. The essence of representation for Sölle is its provisionality. She insists that substitution denies to the person substituted her/his identity and accountability, since the substitute's action is complete in itself, and the one in whose stead it is done has no more to do. Representation, Sölle argues, does not replace the one represented, and so the provisional nature of what is done can be responsibly appropriated by the one on whose behalf it is undertaken.

Where I disagree with Sölle is in my appreciation of how the responses to substitution and representation can be made. In my view, the substitutionary theory of the atonement leaves salvation as an individualistic experience which can only be experienced by faith's completing Christ's work. The cross is defective insofar as it cannot save without personal belief. The representative theory of the atonement does not deny to human beings their accountability in faith, but it presents the death of Christ as effective *de facto*, and it offers a corporate understanding of salvation. Such a view means that

Such a divergence between two main lines of Christian doctrine leads to a difference in proclamation. The preacher who espouses a substitutionary view will be eager to urge repentance and faith in the listener. The representationist will talk of these things as accomplished by Christ and invite the congregation to live what has been given.

I have suggested that the NT speaks of the death of Christ as having cosmic significance. Such a view leads towards a universalist position, and is better expressed by understanding Christ as representative than as substitute. In the context of the funeral, the gospel can be proclaimed, but there will be a determination to avoid using the emotional trauma of bereavement as an occasion of further stress. What can be appropriately addressed are: the reality of death, and the need for separation; the change that the present death means, and the need for transition; the life beyond this death (both for the deceased and for the bereaved), and the need for incorporation.[31]

That is to put it in anthropological terms, but there is more here – the language of conversion in which the old is left behind and the new is begun. In the context of the funeral rites, questions about God, death and destiny can be confronted with hope. This hope will be more than whistling in the dark; it will express a confidence in the cross of Christ as the place where God brings light out of darkness and life out of death.

Conclusion

In this chapter I have offered a theological anthropology which seeks to describe human personhood in unitary terms. I have indicated how this may be applied to Christ, such that his life, death and resurrection are seen as normative. I have discussed (with extended reference to 1 Peter and the ante-Nicene patristic tradition) how the death of Christ means hope for the dead, and how (with reference to two twentieth-century theologians) his death and resurrection are representative rather than substitutionary in their effect.

---

participation in salvation, as Sölle observes, gives the church a representative task role for and to the world:

> "What can be real for us is the actor who plays God's role, the leading player who is followed by many others. What he, the leading player, did – we can do too. Namely, play the role of God in conditions of helplessness. We can claim God for each other. Certainly this play-acting of ours retains the provisional character of all theatrical performances. God, too, is not so fully represented by his representative as to leave nothing of himself still to come. Nevertheless, the identification with God, which Christ ventured and pioneered, means that this identification is at the same time possible for us. We, too, can now play God for one another" (Sölle: 142).

I acknowledge the force of Sölle's argument, and share many of her conclusions as they delineate substitution as an annihilation of the one who is replaced. Nonetheless, my own preference is for J. A. T. Robinson's exposition of the doctrine of representation rather than Sölle's. At least in part this is because Robinson's question is concerned with salvation as the coherence of all things in God. His sermon "What Future for a Unique Christ?" was preached to the Divinity College of McMaster University, the words of whose motto he quotes with approval in his peroration (Robinson, 1987: 14) – *ta panta en autō synestēken* (Col 1.17b).

31 Neither Robinson nor Sölle speaks of representation in relation to the 'forgotten day' of the Paschal Mystery (Holy Saturday). As I hope to show in the next chapter, such an omission in the context of death, bereavement, and the funeral leads to ritual and pastoral awkwardness.

For funeral liturgies, this will mean a twofold agenda. The totality of death can be confronted without qualification, finding its answer in a new creation which is the resurrection of the *nephesh*. Moreover, the death and resurrection of the deceased will be seen as taken up into the death and resurrection of Jesus.

This chapter has offered a theological response to the philosophical question posed by the death of any individual. In the chapter, which follows, I shall propose a theological response to the question of ritual mourning raised by social anthropology.

CHAPTER 7

A Passage from Death to Life

Introduction

In Chapter Five I identified some of the impact that social anthropologists have had on the study of death and its associated rituals. In particular, I described van Gennep's analysis of rites of passage: separation, transition and incorporation. It is to van Gennep's work that I wish to respond in this chapter. I intend to demonstrate how the threefold structure which he distinguished can be linked to the Easter triduum, and in turn how a Christological shape may be given to funeral liturgy.

The common sense answer to the question "What is the purpose of a funeral?" is "To bury Mary". Clearly, disposing of the body is a primary task. However, if there were no more to it than that, we could dispose of human remains by burying them in the backyard without further ado. Yet even when children bury the hamster or the budgerigar in the backyard, there is more to be done than simply making a hole in the ground, depositing the inert body, and covering it over. There is a social ritual. There is a procession to the grave, there is a solemnity either of silence or of words – perhaps of tears, there is a recognition that what previously had life has life no more, and that a loved thing has gone.

I do not want to make any exaggerated claims about the anthropological significance of pets' funeral rites. What I do want to suggest is that, while adult information and suggestion probably support the child in their ritualisation, it is ritual that we require in the face of death.

Social anthropologists have commented in great depth about death rites in primitive societies, and some of the earliest archaeological evidence that we have of human societies comes from funerary sites. Funerals are important since they mark the passing of a human being from the society of the living to the world of the dead. Death is a passage which the funeral formalises. The funeral is, supremely, a rite of passage. In the funeral we may well ask whether it is the dead alone who undertake this passage, or whether there is a parallel passage which the living must follow.

For many people this will seem a strange question to ask. They will see far more clearly the passage that the living traverse than the one which the dead follow. In particular, Protestants will fight shy of the suggestion that a funeral enacts anything for the dead, citing Heb 9.27: "it is appointed for mortals to die once, and after that the judgement." They will mean by their quotation that death ends the possibility of repentance, and hence any amendment in the deceased's eternal destiny. Yet the story in 1 Peter 3 and 4 of the descent of Christ to the dead suggests something different, and is crucial to the *kērygma* at funerals.

The liturgical agenda

I wish to suggest that the funeral should mark parallel rites of passage which the dead and the living undertake. For the dead, the journey passes from life in this world, through death, to life beyond death. For the living, the way leads from life where the departed has been part of their physical experience, through bereavement, to life where the deceased is present by recollection and memory. This parallel passage *motif* is based not only upon the work of contemporary human sciences, but also upon the earlier Christian tradition of the funeral procession.[1]

At the beginning of Chapter Two, I cited the answer of the Church of England's Liturgical Commission in 1965 to the question of the funeral agenda. In the same period the Liturgical Constitution of Vatican II said of the burial rite that "it should express more clearly the paschal nature of Christian death". The two statements are profoundly important in their emphasis on the funeral as an occasion of ministry relating to death rather than to bereavement. While it is the living who gather to form the liturgical assembly at a funeral, it is not they who are the primary focus of what is to happen. This is not an opinion which has been unanimously held at all times among Christians. The Reformers in the days of Calvin and Knox would have subscribed to quite a different view. They agreed that the corpse should be reverently buried, but it was the living with whom they were concerned; they used the funeral as an occasion upon which to warn those who remained of the last judgement and the certainty of hell for the unrepentant.[2]

I have already indicated in Chapter Six that I understand the death of Christ in terms which are more universalist in tone than anything the Reformers believed. My position leads me to take the view that the funeral is more than a memorial of the dead and a warning to the bereaved, although it carries within itself the grim reminder *memento mori*. In what follows I intend to suggest how the Paschal Mystery may be taken as a paradigm of the rite of passage which is heralded in the funeral.

Good Friday and separation

Good Friday is the day of death. It is the moment of separation. However, I do not see this separation as being of the soul from the body. The words of Jesus "Father, into your hands I commend my spirit" (Lk 23.46) express an utterance of dependence upon God, not an anthropological definition. Rather, Jesus is separated from the source of life: "My God, my God, why have you forsaken me?" (Matt 27.46; Mk 15.34).[3]

---

[1]   The processional nature of a funeral will be examined in Chapter Eight, when we will undertake a brief review of the practice and theology of early Christian funeral rites.

[2]   Cf., for example, Calvin, *The Institutes of Christian Religion*, III.25.5.

[3]   Mark's use of Ps 22.1 is taken by some to be an allusive citation of the whole psalm with its optimistic ending. R. E. O. White argues this view ("That 'Cry of Dereliction' . . .", *Expository Times*, vol. 113, no. 6, (March 2002), pages 188-189): "What passage in the whole Old Testament could more fittingly comfort the mind of Jesus in his agony? What but this sharing of the psalmist's assurance that God had not hid his face from mankind, but would yet fulfil his gracious purpose for the world, could explain more convincingly the confidence behind Jesus' promise to the thief beside him of a meeting in Paradise? Or account for the marvellous peace with which Jesus yielded himself to death, 'Father, into thy hands I commit my spirit' (Lk 23.46)".

One religious development within Israel spoke of resurrection as a way in which the righteousness of God could express itself. God could yet act justly even when the wicked appeared to have escaped in this life without punishment and the righteous to have died without reward. It is not unduly surprising to note that the Wisdom movement which concerned itself with this issue of theodicy also re-stated within Jewish theology the idea of the immortal soul. Jesus rejected the Sadducaic arguments against belief in the resurrection, and his confidence was in the God of the living. Among these were to be numbered the patriarchs (Matt 22.32; Mk 12.27; Lk 20.38).

Yet for the pious Jew there was the parallel (if conflicting[4]) belief that Sheol was a land of shadows where the life force seeped away as the flesh fell from the bones. For Jesus, death was not merely a shuffling off of this mortal coil – as it was for Hamlet. Nor was it instantaneously the gate to life immortal. Death for Jesus would have implied the descent to Sheol, where the praise of God falls silent. This is quite a different emphasis from that derived from the body-soul view of human personhood.

When Jesus died, he died completely; and in our dying so do we. We do not have immortal souls that escape the consequences of our human existence. *A priori*, immortality belongs to God alone. When we die, we die utterly; nothing remains. Our *nephesh* disintegrates with the collapse of *bios*. In that dying our ability to respond to the calling of God (our *zoe*) also comes to its end – the praise of God falls silent.

Good Friday demonstrates to us the terror of death in the loss of communion with God. When the Evangelists describe the death of Jesus they speak of the tearing of the Temple curtain, of the sun going dark, of the graves giving up their dead. The death of Jesus has implications for us in the shattering of our religious systems, in the dissolution of the creation, and in the re-awakening of the human past.

In the funeral we need to articulate this sense of total loss. The particular death which a given funeral summons us to mourn is dreadful because it is in one sense the end of the world. Death is one of the four eschatological verities. It calls upon us to ask ultimate questions. For the Christian believer such questions turn us to God as revealed in Christ; and the question of death can only be answered by the death of Christ. In the cosmic disturbances surrounding his death there are clues suggestive to us of how we may deal with the end of the world we have shared with the deceased. As we enter the darkness of death and bereavement, we enter the drama of the cross.

Holy Saturday and transition

The transition which Holy Saturday marks is frequently forgotten in talk of the Paschal Mystery and almost never considered in the context of funerals.[5] Yet it is in this area of chaos and transition that the 1 Peter texts can make their great contribution to the

---

The idea is not impossible – especially since the words are placed in the mouth of a man whose whole mission is the proclamation of God's kingship. However, this chapter follows the view that the cry of dereliction is indeed just that.

[4]   Cf. Acts 23.6, where Paul uses to his advantage the division in the Sanhedrin between Sadducees and Pharisees over belief in the resurrection.

[5]   Not the least of Hans Urs von Balthasar's contributions to theological reflection is his great text on this theme, *Mysterium Paschale* (Edinburgh: T. & T. Clark, 1990).

liturgies of death. The church of the early and medieval periods understood the descent to the dead as the harrowing of hell in which the victory of the cross was effective even among those whom previous ages had condemned. In the total loss which marks the human reckoning of death, there is yet an activity of God which leads to salvation – even in the face of human judgement.

Language about judgement (or, to use Pittenger's language, "appraisal"[6]) is part of what we use when we speak of the dead – even if we adopt the advice *nil nisi bonum de mortuis*. To speak of the dead is to appraise them, to summarise their lives; and we make our judgements as much in what we omit to say as in what we dare to speak. While clergy may rightly wish to refrain from any comment which might be interpreted as speaking the judgement of God on the eternal destiny of the departed, part of the task of the funeral is to address the phase of transition.

At the funeral service the chaotic nature of the transitional is abundantly clear. The reality of what death means is frequently only just beginning to manifest itself. People who have been able to "cope" thus far, or who have really not properly taken it in, are now confronted with the finality of death – especially at the committal. The funeral itself does not mark a distinct hinge between life and death, but it does express much of the ebb and flow between acceptance and non-acceptance that characterises so much of early bereavement.

Failure in the liturgy to express the transitional (however partially) is failure to acknowledge the psychological state of the mourners. More critically, it is a failure to connect death with the new creation in which God calls forth order from the chaos once again. The story of the descent to the dead offers Christian officiants a means of establishing this connection.

The proclamation of the gospel to the dead is a declaration that death no longer holds creation in thrall, for the judgement of God begins with the defeat of death. Death marks our finitude as created beings, but it does not control the Creator. The descent to the dead announces to the disintegrating *nephesh* that there is yet another word to be spoken which inaugurates new life (*bios* and *zoe*). It is the ultimate "word against death". Death is no longer extinction, it is transition; it is, indeed, the gateway to eternal life. This sense of movement from death to life must form part of Christian funeral rites, if they are truly to express the Paschal Mystery and set forth Christ the Representative.

Easter Day and incorporation

A unitary anthropology might lead some to draw the inference that the apparent logical corollary is that the resurrection was a physical and not a 'spiritual' event. However, to describe the resurrection as a physical event is to miss the point. Bishop David Jenkins of Durham was right to seek more than a conjuring trick with bones. At the Areopagus, St Paul talks of the "standing up of corpses" (Acts 17) – the actual phrase is used in verse 32: *anastasin nekrōn*. The phrase makes the Greeks laugh precisely because of

---

[6]   Pittenger, N. 1970. *"The Last Things" in a Process Perspective* (London: Epworth Press).

their body-soul anthropology, which leads them inexorably to contrast the immortality of the soul with the corruptibility of the body.[7]

The resurrection of Jesus is not an act of his own but of God the Creator and New-Creator. In it his life (*bios* and *zoe*) is reconstituted in a new *nephesh*. The resurrection of the body (the *nephesh*) means that out of death we are incorporated finally into God and into the Christ. In the funeral this story must also be told. It is a story which speaks not of survival but of a new order of life whose significance is for the living as for the dead.

The Paschal Mystery is a threefold witness to an eschatology which Christian faith asserts is not merely an irruption of chaos but is of teleological significance. Our end is made part of God's purpose. We must therefore briefly turn to the question of eschatology.

Eschatology

The themes of judgement, heaven and hell (the eschatological partners of death) have been discarded by some as inappropriate categories of thought for contemporary theology. Our world has seen the trenches of the Somme, the gas chambers of Auschwitz, and the horrors of the gulags – to name but some of the hells which visited the twentieth century.[8] Hell is in this life; we need no other.[9]

Moltmann and others have offered us a theology which responds directly to the hells of present experience. God is not seen as impassively distinct from the creation, but entering into its sufferings.[10] Indeed, the *kreuzetheolgie* movement of German theology advances the view that God is most clearly seen as God in the Cross, which is a paradigm for all human suffering and death. In affirming such an understanding, Moltmann expressly draws upon the tradition of Luther's *theologia crucis*.

Process Theology also challenges static understandings of God and one of its exponents, Norman Pittenger, argued very forcibly for eschatology.[11] He suggested that love was not truly love which did not see clearly. God cannot turn a blind eye to what is wrong with things – that would be to sentimentalise God's love; and it is precisely this "appraisal" that gives us the hope of salvation.

Heaven (life lived freely in the presence of God) and hell (deliberate alienation from God) are part of Christian doctrine. We can only ignore their place in the scheme of

---

[7] What then is the resurrection of the body, if it is other than the immortality of the soul? While acknowledging the shift in emphasis, we do not necessarily need to see the body-soul description as inferior to a "purer" *nephesh* anthropology. It is probably better to view the change as an appropriate response to a shifting anthropological understanding. What we have to decide is whether the body-soul view is an essential part of Christian theology, or whether we need to make a fresh appraisal of human existence in the light of our own contemporary scientific and philosophical categories. A full discussion of this issue is to be found in Tugwell (1990).

[8] The list continues in our new century. Readers will have their own lists.

[9] Sartre, *Huis Clos*.

[10] Moltmann, J. 1974. *The Crucified God* (London: SCM Press). See especially pages 211-214 in which Moltmann addresses Luther's *theologia crucis*. From a different perspective the English Anglican W. H. Vanstone came to a similar conclusion in *Love's Endeavour, Love's Expense* (1977).

[11] N. Pittenger, *"The Last Things" in a Process Perspective*, Epworth, London, 1970.

things by altering that teaching. While I wish to re-interpret the tradition, I am unable to change it and remain true to it at the same time. For love to be love there must be a relationship of freedom; and that freedom is a freedom both for God and for humankind. Heaven and hell are responses to the divine love. Love cannot be coerced – even by God, so there must always be the possibility of alienation. To this extent an absolute universalism must, in my view, be modified by divine and human freedom. More than that, I believe, cannot be said.

The pictures of bottomless pits and everlasting fires must point to a reality if they are to be true. But we ought not to confuse pictures with reality: the finest portrait is not the person; the greatest statue is only a suggestion.[12] Funeral liturgies may be able to deal with these issues by reference to our response to the love of God, but we need to be very cautious in the imagery we use – particularly at the crematorium!

Back to the funeral

Can the funeral address the questions of ritual from a theological perspective to which I have referred in any meaningful way? If by this we mean, "Can the funeral complete the rite of passage which death and bereavement initiate?" then I think we must say, "No".[13] However, that would be to misunderstand the nature of ritualisation. What the funeral sets out to do is to rehearse the journey which the living and the dead must travel. It needs in some way, therefore, to articulate a sense of passage even where it cannot itself be that passage in its entirety.

Much work has been undertaken by psychiatrists and bereavement counsellors in studying the nature of mourning and in proposing schemes of support whereby those who are bereaved may learn to live with their loss. We know that the process is drawn out, and most suggest that at least a year is needed to work through this grief – often longer. Whatever the stages and patterns we discern, the categories are not watertight compartments.

All this is agreed, and so much work has been done in this field that the Christian minister is often left to assume that (s)he has simply to apply the lessons in order to get the bereaved "back to normal". Yet there is a danger here. In terms of van Gennep's language of liminality, to get back to normal is to fail to reach the new room of incorporation, since getting back is distinctly different from passing through. The *limen* is a gateway, and Christian faith understands this when it speaks of death as the gateway to life.

There is also a psychological danger in the language of "back to normal". Regression is not a healthy state, and "getting back" (even to normal) may be simply a form of regression.[14]

---

[12] Even among those who continue to express their eschatology in traditional images, there is a reluctance in the conduct of the funeral to consign the deceased to the eternal fire and the insatiable worm.

[13] This "No" perhaps requires some qualification. In societies where death has been privatised, the "No" by and large holds good; in other societies where funerals remain in the public and social sphere and where grief is expressed in lamentation and wailing, the funeral does apparently enable mourners to move into the new phase of life with less unfinished grief.

[14] See also the discussion of regression and rites of passage in Chapter Five.

The world to which we return after Mary's funeral is both continuous with and discontinuous with the world in which she was physically present. For the living there must be a new and radical ordering of living in which *bios* and *zoe* become one. Such a change is what St Paul calls new creation (*kainē ktisis*) and the Fourth Gospel calls being born again (*anōthen*). In calling us to leave the past behind and, even in the turmoil of death, summoning us to begin life anew, the funeral announces the gospel which itself is a call to follow Christ, to engage upon a journey to God.

Conclusion

Death has a social dimension which the funeral must address. The dead and the living make their way to the place of separation. Thence, through the disintegration of the *nephesh* and the turmoil of loss, they enter an arena of transient chaos. Their journey is to a new order of being in which they live in different ways. The funeral needs to set forth this unfolding journey. A Christian funeral will do so by reference to the way which Christ himself has gone, inviting the living and the dead to find their future in the Risen One.

The three days of the Paschal Mystery offer a very convenient vehicle for van Gennep's threefold elements as they are found in funeral rites. Together with the Representative Christology and the exegesis of the descent myth, which I offered in Chapter Six, they form a theological and pastoral basis for future liturgical experiment.

In the chapter immediately following, I shall offer an account of the historical development of Christian funeral rites.

CHAPTER 8

Past and Present

Introduction

The Christian funeral is a call to journey with God from glory to glory. Increasingly, contemporary funerary rites strive to express this sense of journeying through death and bereavement, but with varying glimpses of glory.

The Scottish Episcopal Church in its *Revised Funeral Rites* of 1987 consulted throughout with Colin Murray Parkes.[1] *Revised Funeral Rites* also used material from the French Catholic rites whose poetry and beauty survived their translation into English. Here there is glory.

The Anglican Church of the Province of New Zealand (1989) has drawn heavily on indigenous Maori funerary traditions, and has incorporated them into the Christian texts. The results are magnificent, not least in the rite of the incorporation of the bereaved into new life.

The services for use at and about the time of death published by the Church of England in *Common Worship* (2000) give a clear sense of journey with staged rites provided throughout. There is a wealth of prayers and other resources offered with each service text and the work recovers some of the emphases lost in earlier revisions.

The Roman Catholic *Order of Christian Funerals* (1990) has had its critics. In the main they have been critics of detail – I shall have more general issues to raise in Volume II. However, I remain unconvinced that the rites have handled adequately the ritual element of transition (despite the traditional Catholic interest in this phase of death in its doctrine of purgatory).

Among the Free Churches the Methodists and the United Reformed Church have offered their own liturgical revision in recent years, and the United Reformed Church continues work in this area. The Joint Liturgical Group of Great Britain has also produced its own range of funeral texts. The work of drafting funeral liturgy is very much alive!

This chapter introduces the historical background to the rise of Christian liturgies of death, and describes some of that development from early days to the medieval period.

The historical beginnings of Christian funerals

Christian funerals began as soon as there were Christian dead; however, no liturgies have come down to us from the earliest days.[2] In searching for early clues Geoffrey

---

[1]   See Chapter Five.
[2]   What the funeral of Stephen was like we can barely guess. Presumably in the very earliest cases Jewish rites were used – possibly with the addition of some resurrection hope. Kenneth Stevenson, in his book *The First Rites* (1989) suggests that Stephen's funeral is Christianised by the martyr's dying words "Lord Jesus, receive my spirit".

Rowell argues that there were two main influences upon early Christian funerary rites: Jewish religious custom, and Roman secular practice.[3]

The burial of Jesus is marked by Jewish observance, and it is this mode of disposing of the corpse which Christianity adopted from Judaism.[4] Talmudic and Mishnaic regulations are detailed in their references to burial and mourning, and it is not unreasonable to infer that burial was a most important religious obligation within Judaism. Three stages of mourning were advocated:

–   three days of weeping;

–   abstinence from work until the end of the first week;

–   less deeply formal mourning until the thirtieth day.

The first and second of these are described in Ecclesiasticus:

> My son, shed tears for one who has died;
> raise a lament for your grievous loss.
> Shroud the body with proper ceremony
> and do not neglect his burial.
> With bitter weeping and passionate wailing
> make your mourning worthy of him.
> Mourn for a few days and avoid criticism;
> then take comfort in your grief,
> for grief may lead to death,
> and a grieving heart saps the strength.
> With the burial, grief should pass;
> a life of misery is an affliction to the heart.
> Do not abandon yourself to grief;
> put it from you and think of your own end.
> Never forget: there is no returning;
> you cannot help the dead and can only harm yourself.
> Remember that his fate will also be yours;
> "Mine today, yours tomorrow."
> When the dead is at rest, let his memory rest too;
> be comforted for him as soon as his spirit departs.
> (Ecclus 38.16-24)
>
> Weep for the dead; he has taken leave of the light;
> weep for the fool: he has taken leave of his wits. . .
> Mourning for the dead lasts seven days;
> for an impious fool it lasts all the days of his life.
> (Ecclus 22.11a, 12)

Opportunity for the expression of grief was an intrinsic part of the Jewish funeral.[5] During the return from the grave the funeral procession stopped seven times to provide

---

[3]   Rowell, D. G. 1977. *The Liturgy of Christian Burial* (London: Alcuin/SPCK).

[4]   The reluctance of the Christian church to adopt cremation is linked to the burial of Christ as much as to the negative symbolism in Judaeo-Christian mythology of fire after death. Several rites refer to the hallowing of the grave by the tomb of Jesus.

[5]   Cf. the funeral of Jairus' daughter recorded in Mark chapter 5 – especially verses 38, 39.

for the mourners to be comforted.[6] Yet mourning was not to lead to demonstrative excess, and Rabbi Gamaliel II ordered the simplification of funerals, removing all elaborate and costly show. No Jew was to be buried at a cost which would "leave the poor ashamed".

Important though provision for the mourners is, it is not the central act of Jewish funeral liturgy – rather, it is the *Kaddish* which lies at the heart. This is the oldest element contained in the earliest written liturgy we possess – *Tzidduk Ha-din*.

> Exalted and hallowed be his great name
> in the world which he created according to his will.
> May he let his kingdom rule
> in your lifetime and in your days
> and in the lifetime of the whole house of Israel,
> speedily and soon.
> Praised be his great name from eternity to eternity.
> And to this say: Amen.[7]

Tzidduk Ha-din is a ninth-century work, and is clearly too late to be understood as an influence upon Christian liturgical forms. Nonetheless, it echoes an older tradition of trust in the faithfulness and justice of God both in life and in death. As such, it shows us the roots of the Christian development.

If Christians adopted Jewish practices in funerary rites, it is equally clear that they were also influenced by the customs of the secular world of the Roman empire. By the second century AD, burial was more widespread than cremation, and a common pattern was emerging which J. M. C. Toynbee describes in his *Death and Burial in the Roman World* (Toynbee: 43-64). At death, the nearest relative kissed the dying person in order to catch the escaping soul. The eyes were closed, the body washed and formally dressed (*togatus*), and a coin placed in the mouth for payment to Charon, who would ferry the departed across the Styx.[8] A funeral procession to the grave, dressed in black, would include (in the case of a distinguished man) an encomium in the Forum. Where there was a cremation, the ashes were drenched with wine. The procession would reassemble on its return, to be purified from the contact with death.[9] Later a funeral feast was held at the grave. On the ninth day after the funeral, full mourning was concluded at a further feast during which a libation was poured to the shade of the deceased.

---

6   *Baba Bathra*, 100b, cited by Rowell (1977: 6).
7   Jeremias, J. 1971. *New Testament Theology I: The Proclamation of Jesus* (London: SCM Press). Jeremias (199) notes the similarity of the *Kaddish* with the Lord's Prayer, and comments: "The Jewish community and the disciples of Jesus pray for the revelation of the glory of God in the same words. Yet there is a great difference between them. In the *Kaddish*, a community is praying which is still completely in the courts of waiting. The Lord's Prayer is prayed by men who know that God's gracious work, the great turning-point, has already begun."
8   The *viaticum* in later Christian practice became the administration of the eucharist to the dying. St Ambrose and St Basil were believed to have died each with the eucharist species in his mouth. What was not allowed was communication *post mortem* – this was proscribed at the Council of Hippo in 393.
9   It is difficult to decide whether this rite of purification was in effect a readmission to the world of the living or a final separation from the dead. The later rites may suggest the former, yet ritual washing may well contain a note of initiation and incorporation. Toynbee gives no explanation.

Common to the Roman and Jewish observances are the processional features – even to the extent of feasting. These processions provided opportunities for the therapeutic expression of grief. Yet the early Christian church was uneasy about such occasions, since in the Roman practice such feasts often became riotous occasions, and suggested the sustenance of the dead in their journey. However, this initial discomfort was overcome as the anniversaries of the martyrs were commemorated with feasts and the special days of mourning, adopted from Jewish custom, were given Christian glosses:

–   the third day after death was linked with the resurrection of Christ;

–   where the seventh day was observed, it was linked with the creation stories of Genesis;

–   where the ninth was kept, it was linked with the Lord's appearance to Thomas "after eight days";[10]

–   a fortieth (rather than the Jewish thirtieth) day was more problematic, and different justifications were offered – among them the Ascension of Christ.[11]

As well as the similarity of what we might call the "liturgical rubric" of processions, there was a parallelism in the understandings held by Jews and Romans regarding the progress of the dead. In Roman thought the dead were escorted by the boatman Charon across the river Styx to the realm of the dead. In the Judaism of the inter-testamental period, there arose the idea that the dead were guided to their abode by angels.[12] Such ideas were Christianised and found their way into later Western liturgy in the anthem:

> *In paradisum deducant te angeli, in tuo adventu suscipiant te martyres, et perducant te in civitatem sanctam Hierusalem.*

If we ask about the distinctive Christian contributions which mark out new beginnings, Kenneth Stevenson guides us to Luke 16.22 and its image of the bosom of Abraham. Stevenson observes that this expression is not to be found in Jewish writings, and must therefore be regarded as original to the Christian tradition (Stevenson: 93); along with Stephen's self-commendation, "Lord Jesus, receive my spirit" (Acts 7.59),[13]

---

10   An alternative explanation is given by some Orthodox commentators. They take the number nine to refer to the nine ranks of angels.

11   The variation of custom between the keeping of the seventh and ninth days seems to have been dependent upon local usage rather than on competing theological preference. If the choice had been determined simply on theological grounds, we might expect to have found evidence of a debate within the early Church in which the different positions were hammered out. While it is impossible to draw a firm conclusion from silence, the lack of such a debate seems to indicate either that it was seen as a matter of theological unimportance or of local practice. Since funerary rites were taken seriously by the early Church, the balance of probabilities apparently lies in seeing the two traditions as having adopted local pre-Christian observances for which convenient theological explanations were readily to hand.

12   The development of angelology in the inter-testamental period shows signs of contact with Persian thought, and finds its expression in the apocalyptic writings. The Persian influence is evident in the NT text Revelation 1-3, where the angels of the seven churches appear to bear similar roles to those of the Persian *fravashi*.

13   Whether the echo of Jesus' words from the cross "Father into your hands I commit my spirit" (Lk 23.46) is consciously in Stephen's mouth or Luke's pen, we cannot be certain, but the echo is striking.

this seems to be the limit of our knowledge about the apostolic contribution to funerary rites.

The dearth of other information from the apostolic period should not lead to the inference that funerals were unimportant. The principal issue relating to the death of a Christian was that addressed by St Paul in 1 Thessalonians.

The congregation at Thessalonica shared with Paul the conviction that Christ's return was imminent. For them, therefore, the question of death and beyond was differently expressed. Since the parousia was so close, it might occur before their own death; how would those who had not died experience the resurrection, and how would those who had died experience the parousia? Paul deals first with those who have died; they will be raised. As for those still alive, in language reminiscent of that of the ascension, Paul posits an alternative resurrection in which they will be "caught up in clouds to meet the Lord in the air" (1 Thess 4.17).

As time went on and belief in the imminence of the parousia faded, this language and its implied mapping were abandoned. Yet the central point for Paul always remains: whether we have died or are alive on the day of Christ's coming, we shall always be with the Lord.[14] As he contends in his letter to the Christian community in Rome,

> I am convinced that there is nothing in death or life, . . . nothing in all creation that can separate us from the love of God in Christ Jesus our Lord (Rom 8:38-39).

This concern with what we may call personal eschatology never vanishes entirely. Paul in prison begins to consider his own future and its end in death rather than with the parousia of Christ. In writing to the church at Philippi he frankly acknowledges the possibility of his imminent death. E. P. Sanders considers that the reference in chapter 1.21-25a[15] reveals a conceptual shift:

> We see here the Greek idea of the immortality of the soul, which is individualistic rather than communal. It envisages the ascent of each person's soul at death, rather than the transformation of the entire group of believers, whether living or dead at Christ's return. Without posing these conceptions to himself as alternatives, Paul simply accepted them both. If he died, he would immediately be with Christ, at the end the Lord would return and bring his own, in a transformed state to be with him (Sanders: 32).

It is not immediately clear why a concern with individual life after death should imply immortality of the soul rather than resurrection of the body. While we can agree with Professor Sanders that the emphasis has shifted from the corporate view of the Thessalonian letters, we do not need to accept that Paul has adopted a different philosophical stance – even in tandem.

---

[14] Yet Paul urges his hearers not to be complacent; the imminence of the parousia is not an excuse to withdraw from the responsibilities of this life (1 Thess 4.11-12). In his later letter to the same congregation, Paul underlines the point: Christ's coming means judgement (2 Thess 1.6-10).

[15] For me to live is Christ, and death is gain. If I am to go on living in the body (*en sarki*) there is fruitful work for me to do. Which then am I to choose? I cannot tell. I am pulled two ways: my own desire is to depart and be with Christ – that is better by far; but for your sake the greater need is for me to remain in the body (*tē sarki*). This convinces me: I am sure I shall remain.

This reading of Paul is repeated in Sanders' comments on 2 Corinthians 3-5; restating his opinion that Paul did not see the two views as alternatives, he concludes:

> it is quite possible that some Diaspora synagogues had long since combined immortality and resurrection. In later Jewish and Christian literature they would be explicitly harmonized: at death the soul ascends to heaven, to await the resurrection; at the resurrection soul and body are reunited (Sanders: 33).

It is quite a leap from the possibilities of Diaspora synagogues to a certainty about Pauline teaching, and Sanders does not demonstrate the connection necessary for the inference. There is no evidence that Paul, who addresses precisely this distinction between body and spirit, resurrection and immortality, with his new language of the spiritual body in 1 Corinthians 15, at some later stage abandoned this thinking. He could quite consistently have adapted his eschatology without shifting his anthropological stance.

All that this goes to show is that the practical issues of disposal were apparently not a contentious matter in the earliest Christian communities, but that the fundamental question was one of eschatological concern teleologically expressed.

Post-apostolic developments

Early liturgical detail is scant. Tertullian talks in *de Anima* of an "appointed office", but there is no indication as to its form or content.[16] Eusebius indicates that Christian burial of the dead was a loving rite:

> with willing hands they raised the bodies of the saints to their bosoms; they closed their eyes and mouths, carried them on their shoulders, and laid them out; they clung to them, embraced them, washed them and wrapped them in grave clothes.[17]

Rowell cites a prayer of Bishop Serapion and an apocryphal narrative of the funeral of Elizabeth, mother of John the Baptist, to show that, in addition to prayer and scripture, singing was a feature of the liturgy in this early period (Rowell, 1977: 20-21). Jerome says that the singing of psalms is intended to be a contrast with the pagan custom of weeping and lamentation.[18]

The psalms sung are identified in the record of the burial of the Novatian bishop of Constantinople in 438 as Psalms 22, 23 and 116. While Psalm 23 would be recognised by many modern funeral congregations (chiefly from its metrical setting as a hymn) and the Passover psalm is increasingly being adopted in contemporary funerary texts, the psalm of abandonment would be less commonly known. Chrysostom forbids the use of professional mourners,[19] and the outward suppression of grief is seen in Augustine's bearing at his mother's funeral.

---

16   Tertullian, *De Anima*, 51.
17   Eusebius, Ecclesiastical History, 7.22,9.
18   Jerome, *Ep.*, 108.30.
19   Chrysostom, *Hom. Jn.*, 6.2.

And behold the corpse was carried to the burial; we went and returned without tears. For neither in those prayers which we poured forth unto thee, when the sacrifice of our ransom was offered for her, when now the corpse was by the grave's side, as the manner there is, previous to its being laid therein, did I weep even during those prayers.[20]

There was a determination to avoid in the liturgy any suggestion that death was a finality rather than a transition. The funereal black (or unbleached) clothes of secular Roman practice were avoided since, as Cyprian argued, the dead person now wore the white of heaven.[21] Cyprian stresses the note of joy which should accompany the death of the Christian, as he develops his theme:

Let us show that this is what we believe so that we may not mourn the death even of our dear ones, and, when the day of our own summons comes, without hesitation but with gladness we may come to the Lord at His call.[22]

Two paragraphs later, he writes:

We should consider, dearly beloved brethren, that we have renounced the world, and are in the meantime living here as guests and strangers. Let us greet the day which assigns each of us to his own home, which snatches us hence, and sets us free from the snares of the world, and restores us to paradise and the heavenly kingdom. Who that has been placed in foreign lands would not hasten to return to his own country? Who that is hastening to return to his friends would not eagerly desire a prosperous gale, that he might the sooner embrace those dear to him? We regard paradise as our country – we already begin to consider the patriarchs as our parents: why do we not hasten and run, that we may behold our country, that we may greet our parents? There are a great number of our dear ones awaiting us, and a dense crowd of parents, brothers, children, is longing for us, already assured of their own safety, and still solicitous for our salvation. To attain to their presence and their embrace, what a gladness both for them and for us in common! What a pleasure there is in the heavenly kingdom, without fear of death, how lofty and perpetual a happiness with eternity of living.[23]

The earliest collection of material which gives detailed information regarding Christian funeral liturgy is the *Apostolic Constitutions*. In Book VI, there is a clear indication that the eucharist was celebrated at funerals, following the reading of scriptures and the offering of prayers.[24] In Book VIII, prayers for the dead are proposed

---

[20] Augustine, *Confessions*, 9.
[21] Cyprian, *de Mortalitate*, 20: the brethren "who have been freed from the world by the summons of the Lord should not be mourned, since we know that they are not lost, but sent before".
[22] Cyprian, *de Mortalitate*, 24.
[23] Cyprian, *de Mortalitate*, 26.
[24] *Apostolic Constitutions*, 6.30: "Do you according to the Gospel, and according to the power of the Holy Spirit, come together even in the cemeteries, and read the holy Scriptures, and without demur perform your ministry and your supplication to God; and offer an acceptable eucharist, the likeness of the royal body of Christ, both in your congregations and in your cemeteries, and on the departures of them that sleep – pure bread that is made with fire and sanctified with invocations – and without doubting pray and offer for them that are fallen asleep."

– though how widespread their use was remains unclear.[25] The deacon was instructed to pray for the forgiveness of the deceased and for her/his reception

> into the land of the pious that are sent into the bosom of Abraham, and Isaac and Jacob . . .

The bishop prays similarly, but at greater length, and then pronounces a blessing which seeks for the living that they may

> fight the good fight and finish their course, and keep the faith.[26]

There are also instructions for the observance of anniversaries

It may not be unjust to infer that what is being sought for the living is what it was believed had been granted to the dead. The funeral links the living and dead not simply by the memory of the dead, but by exhortation and example for the living.

Just over a century later another Syrian document emerges, the *Ecclesiastical Hierarchy*, in which the death of the Christian is celebrated as a joyous triumph. The corpse is received,[27] there is a prayer of thanksgiving, and a reading of scripture relating to the resurrection; psalms are sung, then the catechumenate and penitents leave; a list of the faithful departed is read, and the recently deceased is named as worthy of inclusion; those present are then asked to pray for "an ultimate happiness in Christ". The bishop prays over the body and then kisses the dead person – as do all present. There follow chrismation and a prayer for all the dead after which the body is buried in holy ground.

Developments in the East

The development of funeral liturgy in the Eastern Church proceeds from the *Apostolic Constitutions*. Although there are many variants for different deceased persons (male, female, adult, child, lay, ordained, and so on), there is an underlying common pattern:

–   introductory section in the home: prayers, responses, psalmody;

–   funeral procession to church: psalms, psalm-based liturgical chants;

–   service of prayers, hymns and psalmody: normally included two scriptures (Epistle and Gospel), possibly a ritual farewell (last kiss in Greek rite);

–   procession from church to place of burial: psalmody, anthems and responses;

–   burial: prayers of commendation, sprinkling of earth on body.[28]

---

25   See Rowell's discussion (1977: 26).
26   *Apostolic Constitutions*, 8.41.
27   The body of a priest was taken before the altar; that of a monk or layperson was left outside the sanctuary.
28   Cf. Rowell (1977: 31-32). Rowell lists in detail the variant Eastern rites: Byzantine, Armenian, Coptic, Ethiopian, Syrian, Assyrian, Maronite.

The recurring prayer in the funeral liturgies of the Eastern Church is *ho Theos tōn pneumatikōn kai pasēs gēs*:

> O God of spirits and of all flesh, who hast trampled down Death, and overthrown the Devil, and given life unto thy world: Do thou, the same Lord, give rest to the soul of thy departed servant *N*, in a place of brightness, a place of verdure, a place of repose, whence all sickness, sorrow, and sighing have fled away. Pardon every transgression which he hath committed, whether by word or deed or thought, for thou art a good God and lovest mankind; because there is no man who liveth and sinneth not: for thou only art without sin, and thy righteousness is to all eternity, and thy word is true. For thou art the Resurrection and the Life, and the Repose of thy departed servant, *N*, O Christ our God, and unto thee we ascribe glory, together with thy Father who is from everlasting, and thine all-holy and good and life-giving Spirit, now and ever, and unto ages of ages. Amen.[29]

In this Eastern tradition, which develops later in the Mozarabic and Chaldean rites, the movement through loss and grief, which we would identify as a rite of passage for the mourners, is expressed in a processional manner. Indeed, the heart of the Chaldean rite is the funeral procession, which expresses the passage not so much of the mourners as of the dead from this life of suffering and sin to a life of sinlessness and incorruptibility. The body is clothed in the white which speaks of the heavenly garment, and the tone and theme of the funeral liturgy is, in William Macomber's description, "almost uniquely the glorification of God, that is that we may be enabled to glorify him at all times, especially in the face of death".[30]
The rite concludes with a prayer of blessing which rehearses the deceased's participation in salvation history:

> May God, the Lord of all,
> who gave the commandment concerning thee,
> "Dust thou art, and to dust thou shalt return",
> himself call thee
> and set thee at his right hand
> resplendent in the glory of the resurrection;
> and may the Holy Mysteries
> that thou hast received
> plead thy cause
> and win thee pardon at the judgement seat.
> Amen.[31]

The Mozarabic rite places a similar focus on the dead; many of its prayers and much of its worship are addressed to the Lord in the name of the deceased.

It is not that the bereaved are not supported, but their grief begins to be met by its expression in the context of the dead being raised to new life. This is a specifically Christian insight – that the hope of the dead is the hope of the bereaved. The gospel

---

[29] Reproduced *verbatim* in this translation from Rowell, (1977: 54).
[30] Macomber, W. "The Funeral Liturgy of the Chaldean Church", *Concilium*, vol. 2, no. 4, February 1968, page 20.
[31] Macomber: 21.

story finds clear articulation in the ritual observance of death. The last kiss and the psalms of lament display human sorrow; but the Christian determination to see death not as an end but as a transition means that grief is expressed in terms of joy. For the mourners the words of the psalmist are most pertinent,

> He who goes forth weeping,
> bearing the seed for sowing,
> shall come home with shouts of joy,
> bringing his sheaves with him.[32]

The medieval West

The common pattern which develops in the Western church is not in structure so very different from that of the East:

- preparation of the body;
- procession to the church;
- service in the church;
- procession to the grave;
- burial.

The particular emphases of the West were developed from within the monastic rites, rather than by the hierarchical differentiations of the Church in the East. Although there had always been prayers for forgiveness of the sins of the deceased, in the West there was a distinct shift towards a darker portrayal of death. The earlier liturgies were triumphs, now the mood became more sombre; a penal tone was now considered advisable, and the joy of the resurrection was muted – indeed, omitted.[33] With the delay of the second coming, the impact of incorporation into the recent resurrection of Jesus faded. Christians had to live their lives from birth to death with the increasing realisation that their deaths would precede the return of Christ in glory. With baptism now universally administered to infants, the question of post-baptismal sin and accompanying judgement darkened the theological landscape, and death was seen less as a triumphant entry into the resurrection of the Lord. Rather, it became an arraignment at the Great Assize.

One example of this shift is the adoption of the *Dies Irae* into the funeral liturgies of the West.[34] Its inclusion was influenced by the presence of other responses of the burial rites which reflected upon the theme of death and judgement, particularly the *Libera Me*. The *Dies Irae* was not formally in place in the Roman rite until the liturgical revision in 1570, but it had been widely enough used for it to attract the attention of the Reformers. The medieval concern with securing the release of the dead from the pains

---

[32]   Ps 126.6 [Revised Standard Version].

[33]   Rowell (1977: 67), quotes the *Rationale divinorum officiorum* (7.35.27,28) of Durandus of Mende (1230-1296), which notes that funerals should echo the mood of Holy Week when the *Gloria*, alleluias, pre-lectional blessings and joyful responses are all omitted.

[34]   The original liturgical setting of the *Dies Irae* was in the service set for the First Sunday in Advent.

of hell meant that the Requiem Mass took an ever larger place in the liturgy of the dead. For those who wanted to recover what they felt to be the evangelical certainties, in which death marked judgement without any further possibility of repentance, such practices were fit only to be swept away. In so doing, the Reformers moved the focus of the funeral from the dead to the living.

The Reformation

There were two main positions relating to funerals within the Reformation: those who understood burial as a disposal of the body which had in itself no religious import,[35] and those who saw the need for some religious rite in which the souls of the Christian dead might be commended to the mercy of God.

While the former view held sway among some for a while, human need eventually overcame the minimalist approach, and even those most austere in their religious convictions eventually saw the need for some observance. The influence of the separationist view lends continuing weight to many funeral services in the frequent downgrading of the body's importance to which officiants give expression in their attempts to stress the survival of the "real person".

Among the Reformers who did attach religious significance to the funeral, however, there was an equal determination to root out any reference to purgatory: for it was only by grace through faith that God purged and cleansed his church from sin.

The antiphons and psalms were frequently excised, and in their place a sermon was introduced in which there might be "a sincere preaching of the word of God".[36] Services were to be simple and restrained. If the theme of the medieval West had been set by the *Dies Irae*, the tone of the Reformation was reflected by the equally sombre *Media vita* – "In the midst of life, we are in death".

Calvin saw the funeral as the pledge of new life, and urged its solemn performance as an occasion in which all bystanders might be reminded of the truth of the resurrection and so be shaken out of unbelief.[37] This understanding of the funeral as an occasion to sound a warning was softened by Knox, who advocated that the body should be taken directly to the grave, and that the minister should then return to the church to offer comfort to his people in a sermon which talked both of death and resurrection. With this view we see the beginning of the shift in direction which has led to the almost universal assumption that the focus in the funeral is on the pastoral obligation to the bereaved.

The Church of England went through several evolutions as by turn those more or less sympathetic to the Reformation gained ascendancy. The 1549 service is eucharistic, and follows the order set out below:

---

[35] This view is, in a sense, the logical conclusion of the separationist view of death. This earthly body has served its purpose; the soul (or spirit) will be clothed, but in a new body which will be utterly different in its make-up from the mortal coil which has just been shuffled off. All that we need to concern ourselves about is the soul; the body needs to be disposed of, certainly, and burial is a convenient means to this end.

[36] Rowell (1977: 75).

[37] Cf. Calvin, *The Institutes of the Christian Religion*, III, 25.5. Note also my earlier reference to the Reformers in Chapter Seven.

–   a procession to the church or grave;

–   the burial;

–   a short office of the dead;

–   a funeral eucharist.

In the office for the dead, Cranmer drew heavily on the old Sarum rite and included a
traditional prayer for the dead. The continuity with Catholic tradition was thus firmly
maintained.

Three years later, in 1552, psalmody was excised, and the funeral eucharist deleted.
The *Kyrie eleison* and the Lord's Prayer were retained; but prayer for the dead was
scrupulously avoided – it might have had a history in pious tradition, but it had no
scriptural warrant, and should therefore be omitted. The soul was not committed to God,
only the body to the ground. The Reformers successfully exercised a dominant pressure.

Elizabeth endorsed the 1552 order in 1559; but, very shortly thereafter, earlier
tradition was resurgent. In the remainder of Elizabeth's reign only one bishop is on
record as clearly having prohibited the funeral eucharist.[38]

By 1661 and the debate surrounding the introduction of the 1662 Prayer Book, the
Reformation position was articulated in a strenuous effort to defeat the Catholic
tradition. Rowell cites the exceptions expressed at the Savoy Conference (Rowell: 91)
and they are worth setting out in full here:

1.   that there should be a rubric stating that "the prayers and exhortations here used are
      not for the benefit of the dead, but only for the instruction and comfort of the
      living";

2.   that the priest should be free to conduct the whole service in church, and not to meet
      the cortege at the church-stile, "for the preventing of these inconveniences which
      many times both ministers and people are exposed unto by standing in the open air";

3.   that the reference to the "sure and certain hope of the resurrection to eternal life"
      could not be said of "persons living and dying in open and notorious sins";

4.   that the prayer "that we with this our brother, and all other departed in the true faith
      of thy Holy Name, may have our perfect confirmation and bliss" could "harden the
      wicked" and was "inconsistent with the largest rational charity";

5.   that the words "as our hope is this our brother doth" could not be used of any who
      had not "by their actual repentance given any ground for the hope of their blessed
      estate".[39]

Undoubtedly the Reformers and their successors believed that, in advancing these
arguments, they were delivering the Christian Church from unscriptural practices and
thereby recovering the earliest traditions of the faith. Their conviction that death closed

---

[38]   Bishop Barnes of Durham so ordered in 1577. Cf., Rowell (1977: 91).

[39]   Cf. E. Cardwell, *A History of Conferences and other proceedings connected with the Revision of the Book
        of Common Prayer* (1841: 332-333). Rowell (1977: 92) notes that the bishops replied to the second
        objection that it related to tender heads rather than tender consciences and suggested the wearing of
        suitable caps! (1977: 92).

the door for human repentance led them logically to reject prayers for the dead,[40] references to purgation, and funeral masses. Their emphasis on the judgement and the consequent need to repent in "this life" produced a sombre attitude to death, and provoked them to use the funeral as an occasion to preach for the repentance of their hearers. Further, their determination to defend the purity of the bride of Christ – *ecclesia semper reformata, semper reformanda* – meant that they mounted a constant watch on its members.

The old Catholic assumption (monitored by the sacrament of Penance) of the state of grace of all Christians meant that any differentiation in rites was either local or related to the role of the deceased in the Church. The Reformation emphasis was on separating sheep from goats; and while the intention was to assert that this occurred at death and was in the power and mystery of God, the effect was for the local minister (or congregation) to make judgements about who was fitted for Christian burial (and by implication heaven).[41]

The Catholic tradition sought to influence the fate of the dead by the prayers of the church universal; the Reformation seemed to settle the fate of the dead by the decisions of the local congregation.

1662 and beyond

With minor revisions and concessions to the Reformed party, the funeral service published in the 1662 Prayer Book followed the 1549 order. It contained a prefatory rubric which prohibited its use for the unbaptised, the excommunicated, or suicides, and with the ensuing assumption that its use would be for the burial of Christians it reinstated the office for the dead.

Subsequent revisions of the Church of England texts have not raised any further theological issues. Series One was, like the proposals of 1928, a revision of the 1662 text.[42] Series Three and the *Alternative Service Book* (1980) were again largely textual revisions rather than anything more comprehensive – although there was considerable difficulty relating to the inclusion of prayers for the dead. The eventual agreement was to offer such prayers as optional rather than to include them as central to the rite. This was intended to allow for freedom in practice without suggesting compromise in theology. *Common Worship* (2000) expressed its liturgical provisions for funerals with a range of staged rites. Prayers for the dead were again included among the optional resources rather than in the body of the work.

---

[40] Damien Sicard (1978) argues that the Reformation suspicion of the Roman rites of death was misplaced. The old Roman use was simply to sing *Te deducant angeli*. What the Reformers complained of were pre-Christian practices introduced into the Roman rite from Northern Europe.

[41] It may be thought that the Catholic Church's exercise of penance and excommunication amounts to much the same thing as the Reformed practice when the result is that the dead person is denied the benefit of Christian burial. However, at least in the Catholic Church the judgement is made in the affected person's lifetime and there thus remains some possibility in life of amendment. In the Reformed practice, the invidious decision is apparently made *post mortem* with no opportunity for repentance!

[42] There was no funeral rite in Series Two.

Historically, Free Church services espoused the Reformed tradition and shunned eucharistic celebration and prayers for the dead. Funerals were for the disposal of the body, but their direct address was to the bereaved. Informal discussions with Free Church ministers and ordinands indicate a common initial reaction that the funeral is for the bereaved. A very few have said that they believe that it is also addressed to the deceased, but they are unable to articulate how that might be. When pressed to declare whether they consider that a funeral rite can effect anything for the dead, the almost universal response is negative.[43]

In all this revision one ancient tradition has not been revived. The custom of placing a coin in the mouth of the dead for the payment of the boatman across the river of death (the *viaticum*) was, at an early stage in Christian practice, replaced by eucharistic bread. The practice is no longer universally observed; and yet Christ, who is the bread of life (Jn 6.35) is the Word made flesh, who brings us across the stream of death and provides us with bread for the journey. We may well ask whether a Christian funeral rite will not do well to take notice of this, whether in the form of a Requiem Mass or by reference made in the prayers for the living and the dead to Christ as bread for the journey and bread of life.

Conclusion

An examination of funeral liturgies demonstrates that the broad division within Western Christianity between Catholic and Reformation churches holds good. The divergence over how the Church may or may not influence the state of the dead relates not so much to a question of ultimate destination – heaven or hell – as to how heaven may be appropriated by the faithful. By concentrating on that issue, I believe that the more important question is avoided and largely remains unanswered.

"What happens when I die?" is a question which the funeral ought to address. Indeed it is central to the rites of death. The answer of the earliest Christian Church was that the resurrection of the body was guaranteed by the resurrection of Christ. To lose sight of this is to lose sight of the gospel. This chapter has demonstrated that within the Christian tradition death raises most acutely the question of God. Different theologies have offered different answers. All, however, have taken it for granted that the funeral service is at heart an encounter not simply with death as an end of earthly life, but with God.

Volume II will introduce a number of funeral rites and will try to establish how (if at all) they address themselves to the encounter with God and to the issues of theology and the human sciences outlined in the earlier chapters of this volume. In doing so, I have

---

[43] My discussions in ministers' meetings and at theological colleges and seminaries have been by invitation or arrangement, and have been based upon questionnaires designed to test (by the same questions) opinion formed before and after a seminar entitled *What happens at a Funeral?* There has been no real example of anyone at the outset believing that the funeral was only for the bereaved coming to the view at the end that it is only for the deceased. However, while some remain unconvinced that the funeral is for the dead, most take a "mixed" view. Yet in this largest group most feel that their duty to the dead is discharged by a careful telling of the life-story of the deceased. Hardly any feel that there is much sense in speaking for the dead – in the psalter, for example.

had to make a selection from the huge range of available material. To select is to omit, and I have omitted a large number of funerary practices by the choices I have made. My selection has not been capricious, but has been governed by a number of criteria to which I refer at the beginning of Volume II.

CHAPTER NINE

Conclusion

Liturgical texts are not rites, any more than the texts of the playwright are the drama. It is the combination of enacted word, symbol, sign and gesture in time and space which tells us whether or not the liturgy works. Funeral rites are no different from other rites in this respect. When in Volume II we come to examine liturgical texts, we shall need to keep in mind that we are in danger of becoming like the Shakespeare class that toils over "Full fathom five thy father lies" without ever having seen *The Tempest*; we may understand a great deal, but until we have shared in the play – whether as actors or audience – we have not entered that other world.

The best way to talk of funeral liturgies is to attend them. At second hand we can sometimes do this through the medium of television when the funerals of the famous are broadcast. Three such funerals in Britain over a five-year period neatly show the tension between the popular call for a celebration of the past and the theological concern to address life beyond death.

Three funerals

The death of Diana, Princess of Wales, was unexpected. Its media impact was worldwide. A beautiful woman, but wounded by a failing marriage, she had become an icon of vulnerability. At the same time, she had espoused a number of very public charitable causes and protest movements. Her commitment to these was very strong and she attracted attention both to herself and her causes wherever she went. By contrast Basil Hume's death was expected, he had announced his terminal cancer to the clergy of his archdiocese and then to the media months earlier. Although he did not have the glamour of Diana, he had huge charisma and had become an extraordinarily influential figure in British public life.[1] As a Cardinal he was an important member of the Roman Catholic Church and among the European bishops had fulfilled a role of quiet but strong leadership. The death of Queen Elizabeth, the Queen Mother, marked the end of a long life of 101 years. She had gained a strong place in the affections of the British people and had retained it in the public imagination.

---

[1] The legal position of Roman Catholics in Britain is curious. They are, of course, citizens with full constitutional rights in the observance of their faith and in the pursuit of their careers. However, as the law presently stands no Roman Catholic may succeed to the throne. This impediment has implications. At its most virulent it leads to the Unionist politicians of Ulster declaring that "Home rule is Rome rule" as they continue to fight the Reformation battles of the fifteenth and sixteenth centuries. More subtly, it raises assumptions about loyalty. In October 2000 Michael Martin was elected to be Speaker of the House of Commons. It was a matter of comment in the media that he was the first Catholic to hold the post in more than three centuries. What had for hundreds of years been an impediment, no longer was. In no small measure Cardinal Hume's diplomatic skills and personal holiness had created a genuine sense that it was possible to hold a religious loyalty to Rome without in any way compromising civic and national loyalties.

Each of their funerals was televised. Or at least, that was the public perception – a perception which has subsequently led to all sorts of misunderstandings. In the case of Cardinal Hume, the funeral rites were indeed televised. The liturgical texts of the *Order of Christian Funerals*[2] were used, and on a catafalque at the visual centre of the rite was the Cardinal's coffin. In the case of Diana, Princess of Wales, what viewers saw was everything but the funeral rite and the coffin. The coffin was draped in Diana's personal standard with the effect that the harshness of death was hidden.[3] The service televised from Westminster Abbey was more in the nature of a memorial service in which a series of star performances was strung together. In this parade the Archbishop of Canterbury's prayers felt like an intrusion into a showbiz event. Conversations over the following year with various groups and individuals – sometimes prompted by a video recording – indicated three things that stood out in the memory: Elton John's re-working of his song to Marilyn Monroe, "Candle in the wind"; the Earl Spencer's emotionally charged address with its rhetorical gauntlet flung down in the presence of the Queen ("We, your blood family, . . ."); and John Tavener's music, with its slow, repeated Alleluias, played as the draped coffin was borne out by the eight Welsh Guards. The funeral service was read in private at the Spencer family estate in Northamptonshire later that day.[4]

The subsequent implications for the observances relating to death have been quite marked. Many mourners are encouraged to ask for a funeral service that draws on those elements of Diana's funeral that they remember. These they then adapted for their own situation: the recording of a favourite song, the opportunity to make a memorial speech (in which the deceased is usually sanctified before interment), and not too much religion.[5] Christian ministers are being asked to preside at less than fully Christian rites and mourners are surprised when some clergy demur.

By contrast, the liturgical clarity of Cardinal Hume's funeral rites is almost everywhere forgotten. The centrality of the bare coffin continually drawing the onlooker to confront mortality and to see mourning as a response to death rather than as the primary focus of the rite is rejected on psychological rather than theological or liturgical grounds. The persistent note of scripture and the homilist's continual reminder that the task of the liturgy is to set forth Christ as the hermeneutic for understanding human death are ignored in the clamour to "celebrate the life" of the deceased on its own hermetically sealed grounds.

The funeral of the Queen Mother was much less of a media event than Diana's. Her death was quiet and not violent, and the vacuum, which had marked Diana's death, simply did not exist with the death of the Queen Mother. Arrangements had long been in hand, and the Queen Mother herself had had a strong hand in planning what would happen. The pageantry of a full State Funeral did not obscure the Christian nature of the

---

2   *The Order of Christian Funerals* (London: Geoffrey Chapman, 1990) is the revised English version of the Roman *Ordo Exsequarium*. Its approval for use in England and Wales by the National Conference of Bishops was noted in the Decree for Use signed by Cardinal Hume.

3   The coffins of members of the British Royal Family are always shrouded from view in this way; it is a matter of Court protocol and has no reference to any theological or liturgical agenda.

4   The Funeral Service from the 1662 *Book of Common Prayer* was used.

5   Diana's funeral did not begin the trend; it simply accelerated and intensified it, and afforded it some apparent legitimacy.

liturgy. The coffin (like Diana's) was draped in the deceased's personal standard and was borne into the Abbey and into St George's Chapel, Windsor by guardsmen; but this was a much more traditional Christian funeral. The service began with scripture sentences sung by the choir and a bidding prayer written by the Dean of Westminster Abbey.[6] It drew from the 1662 *Book of Common Prayer* and the Church of Scotland's *Book of Common Order* (with its more archaic language than the 1994 *Common Order*). The one prayer from a more modern book (*The Alternative Service Book 1980*) was re-drafted in archaic language to fit with the remainder of the liturgical texts.[7] What was clear throughout was the use of the liturgical provisions of the Established Churches of England and Scotland. The sermon was cast in the manner of an obituary notice with scant reference to the work of the cross and the resurrection, but the remainder of the liturgy emphasised the Christian hope in its selection of readings from scripture and from John Bunyan's *Pilgrim's Progress* and in its prayers, hymns and anthems. This was certainly not a postmodern funeral!

Whatever privileged position the Church may have had in the past in relation to shaping ideas in society – and particularly ideas about the purpose of life and the meaning of death – it no longer holds. Whatever our reaction to the claims of post-modernism that there are no stories giving over-arching explanations of the world,[8] daily observation and experience indicate that those who claim to possess such stories are less

---

[6]   The Very Revd Wesley Carr has written extensively on pastoral care. The Bidding reflected that care for the family and drew on older texts.

In gratitude we bid farewell to a greatly loved Queen.
For her grace, humanity and sympathy,
for her courage in adversity,
for the happiness she brought to so many,
for her steadfast pilgrimage of faith,
for her example of service,
and for the duty which she rendered unflinchingly to her country,
we thank and praise Almighty God.

As we commend Elizabeth, his servant, to God's mercy,
let us especially pray for her family in their loss.

We give them back to Thee, dear Lord, who gavest them to us;
yet as Thou dost not lose them in giving,
we have not lost them by their return.
Not as the world giveth, givest Thou,
O Lover of Souls.
What Thou gavest, Thou takest not away,
for what is Thine is ours always if we are Thine.
And Life is eternal and Love is immortal,
and death is only an horizon,
and an horizon is nothing save the limit of our sight.

[7]   The adapted *ASB* prayer (found there in paragraph 57 among the Additional Prayers) read as follows:
Almighty God, Father of all mercies and giver of all comfort: deal graciously, we pray, with those who mourn, that casting all their care on thee, they may know the consolation of thy love; through Jesus Christ our Lord. Amen.

[8]   In itself, the claim of postmodernism that there are no overarching stories or templates by which we may understand or interpret the world, might be regarded as some kind of overarching story or template!

and less heeded. The Christian funeral officiant may regret it, but more and more people want a Diana style of funeral than that accorded to Cardinal Hume or the Queen Mother.

This book has attempted to show both why there is such a popular longing; most of our contemporaries do not see death as the gateway to eternal life, and so look to the funeral to provide a means of summing up the past. It has also attempted to discover how the Christian tradition may still give an account of death as a gateway. By adopting a theology of the Paschal Mystery as the ground on which to develop and respond to the insights of social anthropologists, we may yet be able to articulate the relationship between life and death whose keys are held by God.

The funeral: an act of worship

Inevitably, much of what the Church does at funerals assumes Christian faith. The liturgies continue the testimony of two millennia to the efficacy of the death and resurrection of Jesus Christ. Yet many who seek the Church's help in marking death do not share even the general proposition – let alone the details with which much of this book has so far been concerned.

To suggest that the funeral is an act of worship will seem bizarre to most people. Death is so final, so complete, that it evokes grief, and grief is not the customary mood for worship. Even when the funeral is perceived to be a celebration of the life of the deceased, worship is not what the congregation may expect. For those who are strangers to Christian faith and the Church, celebration is intended to put the one who has died in the central spotlight. Prayers may be said for peace as a way of calming the pain, but rarely as a wrestling with God (cf. Gen 32.24ff.) – unless the death has been sudden or otherwise tragic.

For some Christians, mourning seems inappropriate. Death is the gateway to life, and so we should rejoice – even in the pain. Those who want to celebrate in these terms explain that they are giving thanks to God for the life of the one who has died. Yet even this apparently good response can bring its own problems. If unchecked, it may lead to glossing over death – almost to the point of denying its reality. It is, perhaps, unsurprising that the Scott-Holland words "Death is nothing at all" are so popular.

The Christian funeral rite has to hold two apparently contradictory views of death in tension simultaneously: death as enemy and death as gateway to life. It does so by reference to two central biblical themes: creation and salvation. The creation stories describe us as made in the image of God. Death snuffs out the breath that God breathed into us and threatens our destruction. The salvation narratives speak of Christ who suffers death but is raised to new life. He is the seed that falls into the ground and yields a great harvest (cf. Jn 12.24).

With these themes in tension (yet resolution), Christians in the face of death turn to God, their maker and saviour. We are made in the image of God (Gen 1.27) and we are destined to be conformed to image of the Son (Rom 8.29). It is Christ who is the firstborn of creation and of the dead (Col 1.15-20) and he represents us to God as surely as he represents God to us. His living and dying and rising are prototypical for us, and so at the great crisis of death we invoke him to lead us in the exodus from bondage of death to liberty.[9] The mighty word that raises him foreshadows that same word that will raise us (cf. Jn 5.25). The baptismal rite that brought us into union with Christ means that we, who have died a death like his, will experience a resurrection like his (Rom 6.5) and nothing – not even death – will separate us from the love of God which we know in our union with Christ (Rom 8.38-39). Our walk through death is not a lonely one, for the rod and staff of the Good Shepherd guard and guide us (Ps 23.4).

This rich tradition (briefly sketched here) evokes in the Christian the response of worship, and that response is so deep that it suffuses death and the funeral liturgies which mark death. It is not inappropriate, therefore, to ask to what extent funeral rites that do not make the death and resurrection the keynote are Christian.

The funeral: a rite of passage

Rory Williams, looking not at African societies but at the people of Aberdeen and North Eastern Scotland, argues that van Gennep's tri-partite model of rite of passage has become less clearly discernible.[10] New rites are emerging, as new needs are being felt and expressed. The principal concern, for many mourners, appears to be more with their own psychological journey than the personal eschatology of the deceased. Their grief does not find solace in belief in a life hereafter; a different strategy is required to deal with those who do not so believe. Whether a theology relying on a unitary anthropology offers any help remains to be seen.

While the Christian content of funerals may be under threat, the processional nature of the funeral may be less contentious – even allowing for the critical analysis offered by Williams. The general public is far more aware than it once was of the psychological journey that grief entails. The rites of death are still staged, even if the formal phases of separation, transition and incorporation are less discernible. The increasing popularity of marking death with memorial services – whether individual or corporate on All Souls' Day or at some other parish commemoration – suggests that journeying provides a metaphor which still has attraction and meaning.

The Paschal Mystery and the other traditional observances of death in the year following are ways in which the Christian community can offer a continuing ministry. Not all want subsequent reminders of the death. For many, the best way of coping is by "not dwelling on" what has occurred. Yet others do find it helpful to have opportunities to reflect at different stages along the way. The funeral service is not the journey, but it may provide a map; and staging posts give perspective and purpose to the new life *post mortem*.

The Christian funeral ought, therefore, to show a way to walk the journey from death to life. In the shaping of its rite, as well as in the content, it will be valuable if the sense of moving on is fostered. Staged rites are a helpful way of expressing this awareness. Stagnation is not an answer, nor is aimless drifting. The funeral, as well as

---

[9]   Lk 9.31, describing transfiguration talks of Jesus' *exodos* which he would accomplish in Jerusalem.

[10]   Williams, R. 1990. *A Protestant Legacy: Attitudes to Death and Illness among Older Aberdonians* (Oxford: Clarendon).

giving space to stop and remember, can offer the kind of direction that will give to the future a purpose and hope.

The funeral: a family occasion

Death is not only experienced within immediate circle of family and friends. In a world shrunk by the television screen and by the Internet, people find an affinity even with the death of those they have not known personally. When a student runs amok with a gun and classmates and teachers are killed, the matter is no longer private. Public death requires public expression of grief. Flowers are brought to an agreed place – often the site where the outrage has occurred, or to the home of the famous who have died.

Yet most funerals are private occasions. Even when a well-known or well-liked person dies, the funeral will be attended by the communities to which that individual has belonged. These may include colleagues and workmates, friends from various local activity groups and people who have had some other close connection. It is unlikely that strangers will be present – apart, of course, from the officiant![11]

From these family members, friends and colleagues, a liturgical assembly must be formed. Those who come may do so from very diverse geographical and social backgrounds. The officiant has to speak to and for all present; that is the essence of the priestly task. Generalities are no longer acceptable (if they ever were); there is an expectation that the funeral will be personal. Family members may expect to take part. At the same time, the Christian minister must not lose sight of the central task of committing the living and the departed to God's mercy and protection.

This becomes increasingly difficult, as the mourners will have seen funerals on their television screens. Whether the televised funeral was that of a real person or of the fictional character in a drama matters little. What is of interest is the psychological tension. The role of the liturgical president is little understood and is normally only of note if there is an error or miscalculation.

Many mourners come to the funeral with the television version as the only pattern they have experienced. This is misleading: death on the screen is at a remove from reality. At the funeral, death is close and at first hand. There is no opportunity to distance oneself, no chance to watch from an armchair with a drink or a meal to consume while the obsequies unwind. The deaths of national figures of sufficient stature to command a telecast are usually marked by funerals that have been well planned by highly skilled people. The funerals in the soap operas can be rehearsed and mastered in the cutting room. When death comes for my mother or my neighbour, there is only one chance to get it right and little (if any) time for rehearsal.

Television makes the remote seem intimate. But the intimacy of a real funeral is remote from what occurs on the screen. The smaller scale cannot bear the polished weight of expectation. Families and officiants have to adjust. It is not surprising that

---

[11] At the funeral of a Member of Parliament, at which I officiated, there were heavyweights from the Labour Party (including the Deputy Leader of the parliamentary party), but such occasions are necessarily infrequent in the general run of things.

there is occasionally disappointment. What is surprising is that it is so comparatively rare.

The funeral: public grief and gesture

The tragedy of the World Trade Centre in New York drew international reaction, as did the death of Diana, Princess of Wales. People express their grief and outrage in making shrines to those who have died. In such circumstances, there is often a move to manage public grief by the provision of permanent memorials. Accusation and counter-accusation drive up the emotional temperature, and it may be that the building of memorials provides a useful mechanism for emotional release – even, perhaps, closure.

Commenting on the Oklahoma City disaster of 1995,[12] Erika Doss (2002) observed how the spontaneous shrine 'Memory Fence' was quickly managed by the city authorities. When the Oklahoma City National Memorial was built, the Symbolic Memorial with its stone and bronze chairs was roped off. Flowers could no longer be left on the site. Spontaneous grief had been politically managed. She concluded that there was a shift in American discourse on death which moved the emphasis from the exclusively medical to focus on a culture in which public art expressed a public response to public death.

> Yet the 'management' of memory at Columbine and Oklahoma City reveals the authoritative religious, economic and political cultures that continue to shape and direct the commemorative dimensions of death, dying and bereavement in contemporary America, subverting the historical realities of these tragic events, and eliding public efforts to change the conditions that contribute to catastrophic violence (2002: 80).

We may or may not find Doss's conclusion is too sceptical. However, public death, whether deliberate or accidental (rail or air crashes, for example), frequently gives rise to public questions. The Omagh bomb disaster in Northern Ireland gave rise to a public enquiry. Among the twenty-nine dead was a woman pregnant with twins; public anger was very high and there was an insistent clamour for information. While this is understandable, it is not always possible either to provide the information sought or from such information to allay grief and anger. One correspondent to the British newspaper, *The Independent*, wrote:

> Sir: What is the point of the Omagh inquest? It is known beyond any doubt how the victims died, where they died, when they died, what organisation killed them and why. What more is the coroner supposed to determine?[13]

Even when we know the answers, we apparently sometimes want to go on digging. The call for knowledge may sometimes be insatiable because it is not simply knowledge but justice (or even revenge) that we seek. The need to know (often expressed in

---

[12] Doss (2002) referred to a number of instances of public death in her paper (delivered in 1999 to a conference in Sydney, Australia, entitled "Thanatographia: figuring death"). Among them was the massacre at Columbine High School, Denver in 1999.

[13] 11 September 2000.

expensive and time-consuming public enquiries) may enable the bereaved to come to terms with the death. But – in its desire to know the cause, to punish "the guilty", and to put right for the future what went wrong in the past – does it also represent a secular version of theodicy? Is it an earthly form of the Last Judgement? If such a conjecture is right, it may be that Christian funeral rites should express a theological aspect of eschatology that expresses judgement in more than crudely punitive terms.

The righteousness of God is not simply destructive. "Righteousness" in the post-exilic prophets and the NT seems to include the idea of "putting right". The eradication of what is evil is undertaken so that what is good may flourish. The cross marks God's destruction of sin and death and the resurrection God's "Yes and Amen" to life and the liberation of the creation. To those who object that evil continues to flourish, we reply that the cross introduces an endgame. The victory is sure, even though its full reality is delayed. We have to take advantage of the crucial move that introduces a new way of living. Revenge simply continues the way of sin and death; one injustice is piled on another. The cross and the resurrection talk of a love that rises from the dead.

At funerals where the one who has died is the victim of violence or of tragedy, the public dimensions increase. In such circumstance, a cosmic theodicy is of primary concern. As Christians, we cannot offer a theology of revenge; we offer the universal implications of the cross.

The funeral: retrospective or prospective?

Donald Gray, addressing the Eighteenth Congress of Societas Liturgica at Santa Clara in August 2001, in a paper on Memorial Services, reflected on the British tradition of post-funeral gatherings at which the deceased's life and contributions to the greater good were celebrated with cheerfulness – and often laughter – lightening the loss.[14] He suggested that in part this arose from constraints within funeral rites which did not encourage the informal and celebratory atmosphere which friends and family often later wished to generate. It may be that the frequently expressed preference for funerals which "celebrate the life" of the deceased (rather than dwelling on the fact of human mortality and belief in the eschatological verities) is in itself a different aspect of the same instinct. The fact that so many contemporary service books offer staged funeral rites suggests that the Christian Church is not unaware of this desire and seeks to minister to it.

Memorial services give the funeral an opportunity to be the funeral. The pressure to canonise the dead before interment is removed from the funerary rite. If funerals are simply the celebration of the departed they are retrospective (with much of the history rewritten in its telling). Where the funeral is genuinely the committal of the dead to God, then a future note will be sounded. What we have been will be measured by God who made us and called us to newness of life.

Gray's suggestion that memorial services offer an informal means of celebrating the life of the deceased not available at funerals is helpful in reminding us that funerals ought to be formal and solemn occasions. Their transformation into celebrations of the

---

[14] See also, Gray, D. 2002. *Memorial Services* (London: SPCK).

life of those who have died endangers that prospective dimension for which I have argued. It is not that we should ignore the deceased, but that their life and our lives are set in a wider context – that of Christ, to whom the Church in its rites for the dead (as in all its liturgies) is bound, and through whom all its prayers are said.

Envoi

This book has been written as an invitation to share in one person's pilgrimage through the landscape of funeral liturgy. Yet like any book and any journey the experience has not been entirely solitary. Others have shared in conversations, others have made the journey, and others have erected signposts and waymarks. Others, too, will follow. There will be better guides, clearer thinkers, more accurate mappers of the terrain.

My intention has been to write not simply for liturgical specialists but for those interested in considering the challenges facing the Christian church in offering ministry in the face of death. Liturgy is more than the texts which it may use. Liturgy is action. Yet the words we use are not without meaning, and they point to the way in which we are to act. Those who minister to the dying and the bereaved must be willing to be silent where words would be empty. At the same time, we have to say something – and we have something to say. As I write these words in the season of Easter, the alleluias resound: *Christ is risen! Alleluia! He is risen indeed! Alleluia!*

I have argued that part of what we have to say and to do remains unchanging. The remembrance of Christ's journey to death and through death to resurrection is at the heart of Christian faith and hope. It addresses those old questions about the purpose of life and the meaning of death; and Christian answers to those questions must always proceed from Jesus' death and resurrection.

At the same time, I have wanted to suggest that part of what we have to say and do may need to change. While the long tradition of the Church has spoken of human existence in terms of body and soul, I am no longer certain that these categories are entirely adequate. I concede that they have a continuing appeal. The deaths of my parents and of my parents-in-law and of many dear friends over the years have not left me untouched by the appeal of the idea of the essential "them" that survives their death. But for the reason given earlier in this book, I have come for myself to reject this language.

Others must judge whether what I have written rings true and (if it does) whether the implications I have drawn follow as unavoidably as I suggest. For some at the graveside or at the crematorium, it may seem that I have made a distinction without a difference. For others it will appear that I have sold a central tenet of Christian faith. One colleague, on seeing the first drafts of my funeral liturgies, could not contain himself. "This is not Christian!", he exclaimed. Others have felt similarly, but have cautiously watched me without anathemas. Yet others have entered into journey with me and stumbled with me. To each of them I owe a debt. To those who have disagreed, I am grateful for the reminder that this is holy ground and not to be trampled upon. To those who have offered encouragement, I am grateful for the reminder that I have not travelled entirely alone.

What now remains is for others to say whether the route I have taken is a good one or misguided in seeking to strengthen the resources available to those whose phone rings with the news that Annie is dying, that George has died, and with the request to come quickly to help. For this is the purpose of our debating: the Church's ministry to those faced with the last great journey.

In Volume II, we shall consider liturgical texts from a variety of Christian traditions and from across the world. In doing so, we shall see how the Church seeks to minister in and around the time of death. We shall look to discover the theology and pastoral care which funerals articulate, both implicitly and explicitly. We shall attempt to discern how changing attitudes to faith and spirituality impinge upon Christian funeral rites.

We shall undertake these tasks in the certainty that, sooner or later, the words will be said for us. In that final journeying, we shall look for the lamp for our feet that is lit from the light of the world. We shall stand and survey the prospect, not in fear but in hope. For death, as well as being final, is the gateway to the immediate presence of God.

> Could we but climb where Moses stood
> And view the landscape o'er,
> Not Jordan's stream, nor Death's cold flood,
> Should fright us from the shore.[15]

---

[15] Isaac Watts, "A Prospect of Heaven".

Select Bibliography of Non-liturgical Texts

A separate bibliography of liturgical texts will appear in Volume II.

Ainsworth-Smith, I. and Speck, P. 1982. *Letting Go: Caring for the Dying and Bereaved* (London: SPCK)

Alexander, H. (ed.). 1990. *Living with Dying* (London: Broadcasting Support Services)

Alexander, H. 1993. *Bereavement: A Shared Experience* (Oxford: Lion)

Althizer, T. J. J. and Hamilton, W. 1966. *Radical Theology and The Death of God,* (Indianapolis: Bobbs-Merrill)

Anderson, R. S. 1986. *Theology, Death and Dying* (Oxford: Blackwell)

Ariès, P. 1974. *Western Attitudes towards Death* (Baltimore: Johns Hopkins University Press)

Ariès, P. 1987. *The Hour of Our Death* (London: Penguin Books, reprinted)

Athenagoras (ed. and transl. W. R. Schoedel). 1972. *Legatio and De Resurrectione* (Oxford: Clarendon)

Austin, J. L. 1961. *Philosophical Papers* (Oxford: Clarendon)

Avis, P. (ed.). 1993. *The Resurrection of Christ* (London: Darton, Longman and Todd)

Badham, P. 1992. "A Case for Mind-Body Dualism", *Modern Churchman*, vol. xxxiv, no. 3: 19-25

Balthasar, H. U. von. 1982. *Man in History* (London: Sheed and Ward, 2nd edition)

Balthasar, H. U. von. 1990a. *The Way of the Cross* (Slough: St Paul Publications)

Balthasar, H. U. von. 1990b. *Mysterium Paschale* (Edinburgh: T. & T. Clark)

Barth, K. (transl. E. C. Hoskyns). 1933. *The Epistle to the Romans* (London: Oxford University Press, 6th edition)

Barth, K. (eds G. W. Bromiley and T. F. Torrance). 1960a. *Church Dogmatics, III.2: The Doctrine of Creation* (Edinburgh: T. & T. Clark)

Barth, K. 1960b. *The Faith of the Church: A Commentary on the Apostles' Creed* (London: Fontana)

Baumann, Z. 1992. *Mortality, Immortality and Other Life Strategies* (Cambridge: Polity Press)

Bell E. 2002. "Ritual Tensions: Tribal and Catholic", *Studia Liturgica*, vol. 32, no. 1: 15-28

Berger, P. L. 1967. *The Sacred Canopy* (Garden City, NY: Doubleday)

Bertman, S. L. 1991. *Facing Death: Images, Insights, and Interventions,* (New York: Hemisphere Publishing)

Bloch, M. 1992. *Prey into Hunter* (Cambridge: Cambridge University Press)

Bouwsma, W. J. 1988. *John Calvin: A Sixteenth Century Portrait* (New York: Oxford University Press)

Bowker, J. 1991. *The Meanings of Death* (Cambridge: Cambridge University Press)

Brown, R. E. 1994. *The Death of the Messiah* (New York: Doubleday)

Brunner, E. 1952. *The Christian Doctrine of Creation and Redemption: Dogmatics Vol. II* (London: Lutterworth Press)

Brunner, E. 1962. *The Christian Doctrine of the Church, Faith and the Consummation: Dogmatics Vol. III* (London: Lutterworth Press)

Bultmann, R. 1952. *Theology of the New Testament*, vol. 1 (London: SCM Press)

Bultmann, R. 1955. *Theology of the New Testament*, vol. 2 (London: SCM Press)

Bunting, I. 1990. *Preaching at Funerals*, 3rd edition (Bramcote: Grove Books)

Caird, G. B. 1976. *Paul's Letters from Prison* (Oxford: Oxford University Press)

Calvin, J. 1962 edition. *The Institutes of the Christian Religion* (London: James Clarke)

Campenhausen, H. von (transl. L. A. Garrard). 1963. *The Fathers of the Greek Church* (London: Λ. & C. Black)

Churches' Group on Funeral Services at Cemeteries and Crematoria. 1989a. *The Role of the Minister in Bereavement: Guidelines and Training Suggestions* (London: Church House Publishing)

Churches' Group on Funeral Services at Cemeteries and Crematoria. 1989b. *Funerals and Ministry to the Bereaved: A Handbook of Funeral Practices and Procedures* (London: Church House Publishing, 2nd edition)

Cieslak, C. 1990. *Console One Another: Commentary on The Order of Christian Funerals* (Washington, DC: Pastoral)

Civil Ceremonies Ltd. 2002. *Civil Funerals: Training Manual* (Huntingdon: Civil Ceremonies Ltd)

Clark, D. (ed.). 1993. *The Sociology of Death: theory, culture, practice* (Oxford: Blackwell/The Sociological Review)

Clark, N. 1967. *Interpreting the Resurrection* (London: SCM Press)

Clark, N. 1992. *Pastoral Care in Context* (Bury St Edmunds: Kevin Mayhew)

Crouzel, H. 1989. *Origen* (Edinburgh: T. & T. Clark)

Davies, D. J. 1990. *Cremation Today and Tomorrow* (Bramcote: Grove Books)

Davies, D. J. 1992. "The Dead at the Eucharist", *Modern Churchman*, vol. xxxiv, no. 3: 26-32

Davies, D. J. 1997. *Death, Ritual and Belief* (London: Cassell)

Dinnage, R. 1990. *The Ruffian on the Stair: Reflections on Death* (London: Penguin)

Doss, E. 2002. "Death, art and memory in the public sphere: the visual and material culture of grief in contemporary America", *Mortality*, vol. 7, no. 1 (March): 63-82

Douglas, M. 1996. *Natural Symbols: explorations in cosmology* (London: Routledge, 2nd edition)

Driver, T. R. 1991. *The Magic of Ritual: Our Need for Liberating Rites that Transform Our Lives and Our Communities* (San Francisco: Harper Collins)

Duffy, W. 1991. *The Bereaved Child: A Guide for Teachers and Leaders* (London: The National Society (Church of England) for Promoting Religious Education)

Dworkin, R. 1993. *Life's Dominion: An Argument about Abortion and Euthanasia* (London: Harper Collins)

Edwards, D. L. 1969. *The Last Things Now* (London: SCM Press)

Enright, D. J. (ed.). 1983. *The Oxford Book of Death* (Oxford: Oxford University Press)

Feldman, F. 1992. *Confrontations with the Reaper: A Philosophical Study of the Nature and Value of Death* (New York: Oxford University Press)

Fiddes, P. S. 1988. *The Creative Suffering of God* (Oxford: Clarendon)

Fiddes, P. S. 1989. *The Christian Idea of Atonement* (London: Darton, Longman and Todd)

Gennep, A. van (transl., M. B. Vizedom and G. L. Caffee). 1960. *The Rites of Passage* (London: Routledge and Kegan Paul)

Gervais, K. G. 1986. *Redefining Death* (New Haven, CT: Yale University Press)

Golding, C. 1991. *Bereavement: A Guide to Coping* (Marlborough, Wiltshire: The Crowood Press)

Goppelt, L. (transl. J. E. Alsup) 1993. *A Commentary on 1 Peter* (Grand Rapids, MI: Eerdmans)

Gorer, G. 1965. *Death, Grief and Mourning in Contemporary Britain* (London: Cresset)

Grainger, R. 1987. *Staging Posts* (Braunton, Devon: Merlin)

Gray, D. 2002. *Memorial Services* (London: SPCK)

Green, M. and Wikler, D. 1980. "Brain death and personal identity", *Philosophy and Public Affairs*, vol. 9, no. 2 (Winter): 105-133

J. Grenfell. 1981. *Joyce: by Herself and Her Friends* (London: Macmillan/ Futura)

Harvey, N. P. 1985. *Death's Gift: Chapters on Resurrection and Bereavement* (London: Epworth Press)

Helm, J. 1982. *Beyond Grief: Coping with the Loss of a Loved One* (Homebush West, NSW: Anzea)

Herbert, C. 1988. *Help in your Bereavement* (London: Collins)

Hick J. 1985. *Death and Eternal Life* (London: MacMillan)

Hinton, J. 1972. *Dying* (London: Penguin, 2nd edition)

Hockey, J. 1990. *Experiences of Death: An Anthropological Account* (Edinburgh: Edinburgh University Press)

Hollings, M. 1991. *Dying to Live* (Great Wakering, Essex: McCrimmons)

Horton, R. A. 2000. *Using Common Worship: Funerals – A practical guide to the new services* (London: Church House Publishing)

Huggett, J. 1990. *Facing Death Together* (Bath: Creative Communications)

Jeremias, J. 1971. *New Testament Theology I: The Proclamation of Jesus* (London: SCM Press)

Jungel, E. 1975. *Death: The Riddle and the Mystery* (Edinburgh: Saint Andrew)

Jupp, P. C. and Rogers A. (eds) *Interpreting Death: Christian theology and pastoral practice* (London: Cassell)

Kander, J. 1990. *So will I comfort you* (Cape Town: Lux Verbi)

Kannengiesser, C. and W. C. Petersen (eds) 1988. *Origen of Alexandria: His World and His Legacy* (Notre Dame, IN: University of Notre Dame Press)

Kelly, J. N. D. 1965. *Early Christian Doctrines* (London: A. & C. Black, 3rd edition)

Kittel, G. (ed.). 1964-76. *Theological Dictionary of the New Testament* (Grand Rapids, MI: Eerdmans)

Knox, I. 1994. *Bereaved* (Eastbourne: Kingsway)

Kramer, K. 1988. *The Sacred Art of Dying: How World Religions Understand Death* (New York: Paulist Press)

Krautheimer, R. 1969. *Studies in Early Christian, Medieval, and Renaissance Art* (London: University of London Press)

Kübler-Ross, E. 1970. *On Death and Dying* (London: Tavistock Publications)

Kübler-Ross, E. 1982. *Living with Death and Dying* (London: Souvenir)

Kübler-Ross, E. 1991a. *On Children and Death* (Berkeley, CA: Collier/Macmillan)
Kübler-Ross, E. 1991b. *On Life after Death* (Berkeley, CA: Celestial Arts)
Leick, N. and Davidsen-Neilsen, M. 1991. *Healing Pain: Attachment, Loss and Grief Therapy* (London: Tavistock/Routledge)
Leming, M. R. and Dickinson, G. E. 1985. *Understanding Dying, Death and Bereavement* (New York: Holt, Rinehart and Winston)
Lewis, A. E. 2001. *Between Cross and Resurrection: A Theology of Holy Saturday* (Grand Rapids, MI: Eerdmans)
Littlewood, J. 1992. *Aspects of Grief: Bereavement in Adult Life* (London: Tavistock/Routledge)
Lorenz, K. 1963. *On Aggression* (London: McEwan)
Lubich, C. 1977. *The Eucharist* (Fakenham, Norfolk: The Fakenham Press)
Lutzer, E. W. 1992. *Coming to Grips with Death and Dying* (Chicago: Moody Press)
Macaulay, T. B. 1985. *The History of England from 1485-1685* (London: The Folio Society)
Macomber, W. 1968. "The Funeral Liturgy of the Chaldean Church", *Concilium*, vol. 2, no. 4 (February)
Macquarrie, J. 1955. *An Existential Theology* (London: SCM Press)
Macquarrie, J. 1963. *Twentieth Century Religious Thought* (London: SCM Press)
Macquarrie, J. 1966. *Principles of Christian Theology* (London: SCM Press)
Macquarrie, J. 1982. *In Search of Humanity: A Theological and Philosophical Approach* (London: SCM Press)
McFadyen, A. I. 1990. *The Call to Personhood* (Cambridge: Cambridge University Press)
McGrath, A. E. 1985. *Luther's Theology of the Cross* (Oxford: Blackwell)
McGrath, A. E. 1988. *Reformation Thought: An Introduction* (Oxford: Blackwell)
Michaels, J. 1989. *I Peter* (Waco, TX: Word)
Mitton, M. and Parker, R. 1991. *Requiem Healing* (London: Darton, Longman and Todd)
Moltmann, J. 1974. *The Crucified God* (London: SCM Press)
Morrison, B. 1993. *And when did you last see your father?* (London: Granta)
Murphy, M. 1989. *New Images of the Last Things: Karl Rahner on Death and Life after Death* (New York: Paulist)
Mury, G. 1968. "A Marxist View of Burial", *Concilium*, vol. 2, no. 4 (February): 79-80
Neuberger, J. and White, J. A. (eds) 1991. *A Necessary End: Attitudes to Death* (London: MacMillan)
Nuland, S. B. 1994. *How We Die* (London: Chatto and Windus)
Ohnuki-Tierney, E. 1994. "Brain Death and Organ Transplantation: Cultural Bases of Medical Technology", *Current Anthropology*, vol. 35, no. 3: 233-254
Otto, R. 1923. *The Idea of the Holy* (Oxford: Oxford University Press)
Owusu, V. 2000. "Funeral Rites in Rome and the Non-Roman West", in Chupungco, A. J. (ed.). *Handbook for Liturgical Studies*, vol. 6, (Collegeville, MN: Pueblo)
Pannenberg, W. 1972. *The Apostles' Creed in the Light of Today's Questions* (London: SCM Press)
Pannenberg, W. 1973. *Basic Questions in Theology*, vol. 3 (London: SCM Press)

Pannenberg, W. 1985. *Anthropology in Theological Perspective* (Edinburgh: T. & T. Clark)

Parkes, C. M. 1986. *Bereavement: Studies of Grief in Adult Life* (London: Penguin, 2nd edition)

Pattison, S. 1994. *Pastoral Care and Liberation Theology* (Cambridge: Cambridge University Press)

Perham, M. 1984. *Liturgy Pastoral and Parochial* (London: SPCK)

Perham, M. (ed.). 1989. *Towards Liturgy 2000* (London: SPCK/Alcuin Club)

Pittenger, N. 1970. *"The Last Things" in a Process Perspective* (London: Epworth Press)

Quinlan, J. 1989. *Journey through Dying, Death and Bereavement* (Dublin: Columba Press)

Rahner, K. 1966. *Theological Investigations*, vol. 4 (London: Darton, Longman and Todd)

Ramsey, A. M. 1961 *The Resurrection of Christ* (London: Fontana, revised edition)

Robinson, H. W. 1911. The Christian Doctrine of Man (Edinburgh: T. & T. Clark)

Robinson, J. A. T. 1952. *The Body: A Study in Pauline Theology* (London: SCM Press)

Robinson, J. A. T. (ed. E. James). 1987. *Where Three Ways Meet* (London: SCM Press)

Rowell, D. G. 1974. *Hell and the Victorians* (Oxford: Oxford University Press)

Rowell, D. G. 1977. *The Liturgy of Christian Burial* (London: Alcuin/SPCK)

Rowley, H. H. 1956. *The Faith of Israel* (London: SCM Press)

Rutherford, R. 1980. *The Death of a Christian: The Rite of Funerals* (New York: Pueblo)

Sanders, E. P. 1991. *Paul* (Oxford: Oxford University Press)

Sandys, S. (ed.). 1992. *Embracing the Mystery: Prayerful Responses to Aids* (London: SPCK)

Scroggs, R. 1966. *The Last Adam: A Study in Pauline Anthropology* (Oxford: Blackwell)

Sennett, R. 1986. *The Fall of Public Man* (London: Faber and Faber)

Sheppy, P. P. J. 1992. "He Descended to the Dead", *Theology Themes*, vol. 1, no. 2 "Christology": 22-25

Sheppy, P. P. J. 1997. "Towards a theology of transition", in Jupp, P. C. and Rogers, A. (eds) *Interpreting Death: Christian Theology and Pastoral Practice* (London: Cassell): 42-55

Sheppy, P. P. J. 2001. "The Dance of Death: van Gennep and the Paschal Mystery", *Worship*, vol. 75, no. 6: 553-560

Sheppy, P. P. J. 2003a. *In Sure and Certain Hope* (Norwich: Canterbury)

Sheppy, P. P. J. 2003b. "Sterbebegleitung und Bergräbnis in der anglikanischen Tradition", in Becker, H.-J., Fugger, D., Pritzkat, J., and Suss, K. (eds) *Liturgie im Angesicht des Todes* Vol. 5 *Reformatorische Traditionen der Neuzeit* (Tübingen and Basel: St Ottilien Press, Pietas Liturgica 13)

Short, D. S. 1992. "The Persistent Vegetative State", *Ethics and Medicine*, vol. 7, no. 3

Sicard, D. 1978. "La liturgie de la mort dans l'église latine des orgines à la réforme carolingienne", *Liturgiewissenschaftliche: Quellen und Forschungen 63* (Munster: Aschendorff)

Sloyan, V. (ed.). 1990. *Death: A Sourcebook about Christian Death* (Chicago: Liturgy Training Publications)

Sölle, D. 1967. *Christ the Representative: An Essay in Theology after the "Death of God"* (London: SCM Press)

Speck, P. 1988. *Being There: Pastoral Care in Time of Illness* (London: SPCK)

Spinks, B. D. 1999. "Ecclesiology and Soteriology shaping Eschatology", in Spinks, B. D. and Torrance I. R. (eds) *To Glorify God* (Edinburgh: T. & T. Clark)

Spufford, M. 1989. *Celebration* (London: Collins/Fount)

Stauffer, E. 1963. *New Testament Theology* (London: SCM Press)

Stedeford, A. 1984. *Facing Death: Patients, Families and Professionals* (Oxford: Heinemann)

Stevenson, K. W. 1989. *The First Rites: Worship in the Early Church* (London: Marshall Pickering)

Stroebe, M. S., Stroebe W. and Hansson, R. O. (eds) 1993 *Handbook of Bereavement: Theory, Research, and Intervention* (Cambridge: Cambridge University Press)

Swinburne, R. W. 1996. *Is there a God?* (Oxford: Oxford University Press)

Taylor, R. B. 1980. *Cultural Ways* (Boston, MA: Ally and Bacon, 3rd edition)

Thielicke, H. 1964. *How The World Began* (London: James Clarke)

Tillich, P. 1978. *Systematic Theology* (London: SCM Press)

Toynbee, J. M. C. 1971. *Death and Burial in the Roman World* (London: Thames and Hudson)

Tugwell, S. 1990. *Human Immortality and the Redemption of Death* (London: Darton, Longman and Todd)

Turner, V. 1969. *The Ritual Process: Structure and Anti-Structure* (Chicago: Aldine)

Vanstone, W. H. 1977. *Love's Endeavour, Love's Expense: The Response of Being to the Love of God* (London: Darton, Longman and Todd)

Velkovska, E. V. 2000. "Funeral Rites in the East", in Chupungco, A. J. (ed.). *Handbook for Liturgical Studies*, vol. 6 (Collegeville, MN: Pueblo)

Vizedom, M. B. 1976. *Rites and Relationships: Rites of Passage and Contemporary Anthropology* (Beverley Hills, CA: Sage)

Walker, M. 1989. *The God of our Journey* (London: Marshall Pickering)

Wallbank, S. 1991. *Facing Grief: bereavement and the young adult* (Cambridge: Lutterworth)

Wallbank, S. 1992. *The Empty Bed: Bereavement and the Loss of Love* (London: Darton, Longman and Todd)

Walter, J. A. 1990. *Funerals – And How To Improve Them* (London: Hodder and Stoughton)

Whitaker, A. (ed.). 1984. *All in the End is Harvest: An Anthology for those who Grieve* (London: Darton, Longman and Todd)

White, R. E. O. 2002. "That 'Cry of Dereliction' . . .", *Expository Times*, vol. 113, no. 6: 188-189

White, V. 1991. *Atonement and Incarnation: An Essay in Universalism and Particularity* (Cambridge: Cambridge University Press)

Wilkinson, T. 1991. *The Death of a Child: A Book for Families* (London: Julia Macrae)

Williams, R. 1990. *A Protestant Legacy: Attitudes to Death and Illness among Older Aberdonians* (Oxford: Clarendon)

Willson, J. W. 1989. *Funerals without God: A Practical Guide to Non-religious Funerals* (London: British Humanist Association)

Wolff, H. W. (transl. M. Kohl). 1974. *Anthropology of the Old Testament* (London: SCM Press)

Woodward, J. (ed.). 1990. *Embracing the Chaos: Theological Responses to Aids* (London: SPCK)

Worden, J. W. 1991. *Grief Counselling and Grief Therapy: A Handbook for the Mental Health Practitioner* (London: Tavistock Routledge, 2nd edition)

Young, F. 1990. *Face to Face: A narrative essay in the theology of suffering* (Edinburgh: T. & T. Clark)

Zaleski, C. 1987. *Otherworld Journeys: Accounts of Near-Death Experience in Medieval and Modern Times* (Oxford: Oxford University Press)

Index of Scripture Passages

A separate Index of Scripture Passages appears in Volume II.

Index of Names

A separate Index of Names appears in Volume II.

Index of Names

General Index

A separate General Index appears in Volume II.